Making Sense of Administrative Leadership:
The 'L' Word in Higher Education

by Estela M. Bensimon, Anna Neumann, and Robert Birnbaum

ASHE-ERIC Higher Education Report 1, 1989

Prepared by

Clearinghouse on Higher Education
The George Washington University

In cooperation with

ASHE

Association for the Study
of Higher Education

Published by

School of Education and Human Development
The George Washington University

Jonathan D. Fife, Series Editor

Cite as
Bensimon, Estela M., Anna Neumann, and Robert Birnbaum.
*Making Sense of Administrative Leadership: The 'L' Word in
Higher Education.* ASHE-ERIC Higher Education Report No.
1. Washington, D.C.: School of Education and Human Devel-
opment, The George Washington University, 1989.

Library of Congress Catalog Card Number 89-62601
ISSN 0884-0040
ISBN 0-9623882-0-3

Managing Editor: Christopher Rigaux
Manuscript Editor: Barbara Fishel/Editech
Cover design by Michael David Brown, Rockville, Maryland

The ERIC Clearinghouse on Higher Education invites individuals to submit proposals for writing monographs for the
ASHE-ERIC Higher Education Report series. Proposals must
include:
1. A detailed manuscript proposal of not more than five pages.
2. A chapter-by-chapter outline.
3. A 75-word summary to be used by several review committees for the initial screening and rating of each proposal.
4. A vita and a writing sample.

ERIC **Clearinghouse on Higher Education**
School of Education and Human Development
The George Washington University
One Dupont Circle, Suite 630
Washington, DC 20036-1183

This publication was prepared partially with funding from
the Office of Educational Research and Improvement, U.S.
Department of Education, under contract no. ED RI-88-062014.
The opinions expressed in this report do not necessarily
reflect the positions or policies of OERI or the Department.

EXECUTIVE SUMMARY

Why Do We Need Leadership?

A perception exists that higher education is experiencing a "great leadership crisis." Calls for better, stronger, more visionary, and bolder leadership intensified after the publication of several reports by blue ribbon commissions, whose running theme is "the decline of higher education." *To Reclaim a Legacy* (Bennett 1984) challenges presidents to be more courageous in assuming the role of leadership in curricular reform. And *Integrity in the College Curriculum* declares that "this generation of academic presidents and deans is required to lead us away from the declining and devalued bachelor's degree" (AAC 1985, p. 7).

The message in these and other reports on the state of higher education is that official campus leaders—presidents and other academic officers—need to direct and guide their campuses if the problems of higher education are to be confronted and resolved. This faith in the power and wisdom of leadership and its potential to make a difference in colleges and universities underlies much of the literature of higher education and is particularly ubiquitous in contemporary and highly popular works on leadership. Recently, however, scholars have posited new ideas that challenge traditional notions that organizations are driven by leadership or that the quality of leadership significantly affects organizational performance.

What Is Leadership?

Research traditions in leadership can be grouped into six major categories: *trait theories,* which attempt to identify specific personal characteristics that appear to contribute to a person's ability to assume and successfully function in positions of leadership; *power and influence theories,* which consider leadership in terms of the source and amount of power available to leaders and the manner in which leaders exercise that power over followers through either unilateral or reciprocal interactions; *behavioral theories,* which study leadership by examining patterns of activity, managerial roles, and behavior categories of leaders—that is, by considering what it is that leaders actually *do; contingency theories,* which emphasize the importance of situational factors, such as the nature of the task performed by a group or the nature of the external environment to understand effective leadership; *cultural and symbolic theories,* which study the influence of leaders in maintaining or reinterpreting the systems of shared beliefs and values that give meaning to organizational life; and *cognitive theories,* which suggest leadership is a social attribution that permits people to make sense of an equivocal, fluid, and complex world.

One of the most useful organizational typologies from the perspective of leadership suggests that organizations can be looked at through four different vantage points or coherent perspectives, identified as "frames" (Bolman and Deal 1984). The *structural frame* emphasizes formal roles and relationships, the *human resource frame* focuses on the needs of people, the *political frame* considers the conflict over scarce resources, and the *symbolic frame* views organizations as cultures with shared values.

Is Leadership in Higher Education Different?

Even though the literature on leadership and organizational theory is rich, its many conceptual orientations and interpretations do not appear to be particularly influential, at least not explicitly, in informing the literature on administrative leadership in higher education. Much of this work tends to be atheoretical, with considerable attention given to style of leadership and personality traits.

The study of leadership in colleges and universities is problematic because of the dual control systems, conflicts between professional and administrative authority, unclear goals, and other special properties of normative, professional organizations. Leadership in higher education can be examined from the perspective of leadership theories and organizational frames, however, even though an explicit conceptual orientation is absent in many of the works.

Research and commentaries on the presidency suggest that presidents tend to accept a traditional and directive view when they define their leadership role; few appear to emphasize the importance of two-way communication or social exchange processes of mutual influence or to identify leadership as facilitating rather than directing the work of highly educated professionals. Furthermore, few works have considered the possibility that the debate about transformational versus transactional may not be purely an "either/or" and that both perspectives may be useful but in a more complex configuration.

How Are Our Views of Leadership Changing?

Several contemporary works indicate that the understanding of leadership in academic organizations, at least among scholars, may be undergoing a paradigmatic shift, from a rational perspective toward a cultural and symbolic perspective. Close attention is being given to the manifestation of symbolic leadership, as shown by works concerning the role of college presidents in the management of meaning, the construction of institutional reality, and the interpretation of myths, rituals, and symbols. For the most part, however, cultural and symbolic views of leadership have not been incorporated into the practitioners' perspective of higher education administration, perhaps because it tends to present the leader in a role that is considerably more modest than seen in images of heroic or transformational leadership associated with rational and power-based theories.

Cultural and symbolic theories deserve serious attention because they present a view of leadership that is highly compatible with the characteristics of academic organizations. The ambiguity of purpose, the diffusion of power and authority, and the absence of clear and measurable outcomes are but a few of the constraints faced by college presidents and other administrative leaders. Viewed from a rational perspective, these constraints make the presidency appear as an impossible job. Presidents who consider their role from a symbolic perspective will be less concerned about displaying bold leadership to leave their imprint on a campus, more concerned with making marginal improvements and helping campus constituents make sense of an equivocal world.

ADVISORY BOARD

Roger G. Baldwin
Assistant Professor of Education
College of William and Mary

Carol M. Boyer
Consultant and Senior Academic Planner
Massachusetts Board of Regents of Higher Education

Ellen Earle Chaffee
Associate Commissioner of Academic Affairs
North Dakota State Board of Higher Education

Elaine H. El-Khawas
Vice President, Policy Analysis and Research
American Council on Education

Martin Finkelstein
Associate Professor of Higher Education Administration
Seton Hall University

Carol Everly Floyd
Associate Vice Chancellor for Academic Affairs
Board of Regents of the Regency Universities System
State of Illinois

George D. Kuh
Professor of Higher Education
Indiana University

Yvonna S. Lincoln
Associate Professor of Higher Education
University of Kansas

Richard F. Wilson
Associate Chancellor
University of Illinios

Ami Zusman
Principal Analyst, Academic Affairs
University of California

CONSULTING EDITORS

Robert J. Barak
Deputy Executive Secretary
Director of Academic Affairs and Research
Iowa Board of Regents

Robert Berdahl
Professor of Higher Education
University of Maryland

Kenneth A. Bruffee
Director, The Scholars Program
Brooklyn College of the City of New York

L. Leon Campbell
Provost and Vice President for Academic Affairs
University of Delaware

Robert Paul Churchill
Chair and Associate Professor
Department of Philosophy
The George Washington University

Charles S. Claxton
Associate Professor
Center for the Study of Higher Education
Memphis State University

Susan Cohen
Associate, Project for Collaborative Learning
Lesley College

John W. Creswell
Professor and Lilly Project Director
University of Nebraska

Andre Deruyttere
Vice President
Catholic University at Leuven, Belgium

Irwin Feller
Director, Institute for Policy Research and Evaluation
Pennsylvania State University

Zelda F. Gamson
Director
New England Resource Center for Higher Education

Kenneth C. Green
Associate Director
Higher Education Research Institute
University of California at Los Angeles

Milton Greenberg
Provost
American University

Judith Dozier Hackman
Associate Dean
Yale University

Brian L. Hawkins
Vice President for Computing and Information Sciences
Brown University

Lynn G. Johnson
Executive Director
Hudson-Mohawk Association of Colleges and Universities

Carl J. Lange
Professor Emeritus
The George Washington University

Oscar T. Lenning
Vice President for Academic Affairs
Robert Wesleyan College

Judith B. McLaughlin
Research Associate on Education and Sociology
Harvard University

Andrew T. Masland
Judicial/Public Safety Market Manager
Digital Equipment Corporation

Marcia Mentkowski
Director of Research and Evaluation
Professor of Psychology
Alverno College

Richard I. Miller
Professor of Higher Education
Ohio University

James R. Mingle
Executive Director
State Higher Education Executive Officers

Elizabeth M. Nuss
Executive Director
National Association of Student Personnel Administrators

Anne M. Pratt
Director for Foundation Relations
College of William and Mary

Karen T. Romer
Associate Dean for Academic Affairs
Brown University

Jack E. Rossman
Professor of Psychology
Macalester College

Mary Ann Sheridan
Director of Sponsored Programs
Ohio State University Research Foundations

J. Fredericks Volkwein
Director of Institutional Research
State University of New York at Albany

William R. Whipple
Director, Honors Program
University of Maine

CONTENTS

FOREWORD

The following three statements are probably universally accepted as truths: There is a general consensus that higher education has a leadership crisis. Strong, effective leadership is necessary for a strong, effective institution. Most academic leaders are unschooled and unsure about what comprises effective leadership.

A report that simply reviews the theoretical literature on leadership will not fill this higher education leadership vacuum. The major scholarly work on leadership has been conducted in the area of political science and business administration. There is a serious concern on the applicability of this literature as it relates to non-profit, professional organizations such as colleges and universities. What is needed is a careful integration and synthesis of this literature base with the literature concerning higher education as a social institution. This has been magnificently done by Estela Bensimon of Pennsylvania State University, Anna Neumann of Columbia University, and Robert Birnbaum of the University of Maryland. In this report, the authors have reviewed the literature that gives a "conceptual explanation" of leadership. They then relate this literature directly to higher education and its sociological and organizational uniqueness. Their final integration of this literature develops a clarity concerning higher education leadership. It will have major impact in the understanding of higher education leadership for many years to come.

Leadership is not only a process, it is a value. In organizations, such as higher education, that are primarily value-driven, an understanding of leadership at all levels is crucial for the effectiveness of the organization. It is critical to what the organization is. How people value leadership is very crucial to the make-up and dynamics of what that organization will become. There is no right or correct leadership process. What is wrong is for any organization to develop leadership practices through ignorance. This report can help to enlighten those that are willing to be helped.

Jonathan D. Fife
Professor and Director
ERIC Clearinghouse on Higher Education
School of Education and Human Development
The George Washington University

ACKNOWLEDGMENTS

We would like to acknowledge several important sources of financial, administrative, and intellectual support in completing this monograph. We are grateful to the Office for Educational Research and Improvement/Department of Education (OERI/ED), the Lilly Endowment, and TIAA-CREF for supporting our work on institutional leadership. We are especially grateful to Eleanor Fujita, who was responsible for preparing the bibliography and ensuring the accuracy of citations. Without her initiative, creativity, and dedication our task would have been infinitely more difficult and considerably less pleasant. We also wish to thank Jeanine L. Marquart for organizing our materials on leadership into a highly professional library. We would like to thank Ellen Earle Chaffee of the North Dakota State Board of Higher Education, and our colleagues at the National Center for Postsecondary Governance and Finance, Richard C. Richardson and Kathryn Theus for their careful reading and numerous suggestions for improvement. We also wish to acknowledge the helpful comments made by several anonymous reviewers.

Concern with institutional leadership has increased in recent years. This attention is in part related to a perception that higher education is experiencing a "great leadership crisis." According to *Academic Strategy,* one of the most widely read books about higher education, "one of the most significant developments in postwar academic life has been the progressive breakdown of governance and leadership" (Keller 1983, p. 27). The author is not alone in perceiving a "crisis of leadership" in higher education.

As the 1980s have become the era of criticism, leadership correspondingly has been touted as the cure for higher education's ills.

Calls for better, stronger, and bolder leadership have been echoed simultaneously in several reports by blue ribbon commissions, decrying the decline of higher education. In *To Reclaim a Legacy* (Bennett 1984), former Secretary of Education William Bennett challenges college presidents to be more courageous in assuming a leadership role in curricular reform, suggesting that the revitalization of colleges and universities depends on presidents who are willing to assume a strong role in the academic affairs of their institutions, just as effectiveness in elementary and secondary schools depends upon strong school principals. In a similar but stronger tone, *Integrity in the College Curriculum* (AAC 1985) blames the disintegration of the curriculum on faculty, declaring that the crisis will only grow unless presidents reassert their leadership for the curriculum and shape a strategy to move their faculties to responsible action. The mandate being handed to official campus leaders contains no hint of ambivalence:

> *This generation of academic presidents and deans is required to lead us away from the declining and devalued bachelor's degree. . . . Their visions must be bolder, their initiatives more energetic and imaginative, and the great potential for academic leadership that is latent in the authority of their positions must be asserted forcefully and skillfully* (p. 7).

Thus, as the 1980s have become the era of criticism, leadership correspondingly has been touted as the cure for higher education's ills. The message resounds that campus leaders— presidents and other academic officers—should take action to resolve problems contributing to higher education's demise. This faith in the power and wisdom of leadership and in its potential to make a difference in colleges and universities underlies much of the literature of higher education.

It is particularly ubiquitous in contemporary and highly popular works on leadership. Some suggest, for example, that every organization "must have a single authority, someone or some body of people authorized to initiate, plan, decide, manage, monitor, and punish its members" and that "leadership is imperative" to accomplish this end (Keller 1983, p. 35). Another observer calls for "strong, assertive, and enlightened presidents who will lead us to a new and higher level of contribution" (Fisher 1984, p. 11), while yet another asserts that leadership is both necessary and important because people instinctively want to have leaders, because groups need leaders to perform functions that groups cannot perform for themselves, and because leaders can provide an effective check on "unseen players" who might manipulate power to the detriment of the group (Gardner 1986b, p. 19). And the national best-seller, *In Search of Excellence: Lessons from America's Best-Run Companies,* stresses the central importance of the leader, who is "the value shaper, the exemplar, the maker of meanings" in converting average companies and average employees into excellent organizations (Peters and Waterman 1982, p. 82).

Constraints in Responding to the Calls for Leadership

Although calls for leadership abound and although optimism runs high at the thought of finding new, vigorous, decisive, transforming, and inspirational leaders, few are consistent with normative statements describing how college and university leadership and governance should ideally function. Governance is not solely an administrative prerogative but properly is a shared responsibility and joint effort involving all important campus constituencies, particularly the faculty.

The influential "Joint Statement on Government of Colleges and Universities," for example, bestows on the faculty the primary responsibility for "curriculum, subject matter and methods of instruction, research, faculty status, and those aspects of student life [that] relate to the educational process" (American Association of University Professors 1984, p. 109). In such matters, the president is expected to "concur with the faculty judgment except in rare instances and for compelling reasons, which should be stated in detail" (p. 109). In sum, the Joint Statement reserves for faculty authority over the central function of colleges and universities. Thus, reformist reports of the 1980s calling for strong and courageous leadership may be dysfunctional by AAUP standards, if not impossible. The norms of the profession may militate against the kinds of assertive leadership that has been called for because change would require faculty, administrators, and trustees to act—and to allow each other to act—in ways that radically depart from strongly ingrained beliefs as to the proper role of the administration and the faculty.

Although presidents and administrators may do all the "right things" as prescribed in the calls for leadership, they may still fail in the end if their initiatives do not coincide with desires of faculties, trustees, or other key constituencies. While presidents are being counseled to "turn their institutions around," evidence suggests that acting too fast and too aggressively may cause contentious relationships between faculty and administration, which in some cases could result in dismissal or premature departure from the presidency (Biemiller 1986; Mooney 1988). Faculty expectations for involvement in decision making may represent the single greatest obstacle to directive leadership.

Reports and commentaries in *The Chronicle of Higher Education* have addressed pressures on college leaders, especially on presidents, in attending simultaneously to external audiences to raise funds and friends and in responding to calls for accountability (Evangelauf 1984); in shaping trustees' leadership so that it avoids extremes of nonparticipation and overparticipation (Jacobson 1985); in attending simultaneously to boards that want a role in internal college management and faculties that want to be consulted on personnel appointments and financial decisions (McMillen 1986); and in using the thinking of the marketplace, without sounding like "heads of automobile dealerships" or without forgetting education's fundamental mission (Plante 1985). The professional media are rife with pictures of college presidents caught among the conflicting ideals, standards, expectations, and demands of faculty, trustees, students, community, state agencies, and interest groups.

Furthermore, several external and internal constraints and pressures have been identified that reduce the degrees of freedom within which college presidents exercise leadership, including reduced confidence in leadership and respect for authority; reduced institutional growth resulting from demographic changes in the student body and declining resources; intrusion of external groups, such as the media and government (e.g., sunshine laws, legal action); the need to contend with system bureaucracies, faculty unions, and intrusive boards of trustees; and the presence of friends, colleagues, and associates who can turn as easily into fatal opponents (Kerr and Gade 1986).

One of the dilemmas faced by college presidents is that soon after assuming office, they learn it is very difficult to leave their mark on the institution (Kauffman 1980). Campus expectations strongly influence what the president can realistically accomplish. Often presidents become caught up in counteracting their predecessors' actions, ministering to a divided campus or correcting budgetary deficiencies. The extent to which presidents can lead vigorously may be severely limited by institutional history as well as by an established constituency that can as easily welcome as reject bold attempts at reform. Given these realities, most presidents accept that their impact may be equivocal.

Overcoming Constraints to Leadership

Critics of higher education leadership seem to assume that today's presidents do not have the courage and decisiveness of past presidents. An obvious solution would be for presidential search committees to seek stronger and more decisive candidates. Alternatively, the presidency could be strengthened by increasing the legal authority of the position and curtailing the influence of other groups. A former president (Fisher 1984) proposed that trustees should consider suspending all existing college policies regarding shared authority and grant exclusive authority to the president for the conduct of all campus affairs. The president could then give other campus groups, as a privilege, the opportunity to participate in governance at the president's discretion. A less radical proposal would give presidents greater discretion to act without the full panoply of consultation and consensus building, while requiring accountability through periodic reviews of their performance (Brewster 1976; Mortimer and McConnell 1978).

Presidents have resources at their disposal with which they can exercise their influence, including substantial control over the budget, extensive staffs, and presidential authority to appoint key personnel and to set institutional priorities (Corson 1960; Trow 1984). Nevertheless, these resources may be illusory (Cohen and March 1974). For example, accounting procedures may constrain how much influence presidents have on budgetary decision making, decisions about the curriculum and academic appointments are delegated to the faculty, and planning activities have greater symbolic than instrumental value.

One special resource—the governing board's support—has been given extensive attention. It has been said that the ability of today's college president to lead in the face of seemingly overwhelming constraints requires, first and foremost, the board's commitment to create an effective presidency (Kerr 1984), which requires the board to review the presidency regularly (for example, as part of a regular governance review), include the president as a board member (or accord membership when full membership is prohibited by law), provide for an adequate presidential staff and a top leadership team, uphold the president's role as the institution's chief academic officer, approve union contracts as advised by the president and avoid pitting the president directly against union officials during negotiations, provide the president with discretionary resources to initiate innovative programs, and build a board of devoted trustees whose terms are long enough to permit good working relationships to be established and substantive projects to be accomplished. Thus, it is possible for boards to ease constraints on presidential leadership.

The realization that leadership must be practiced in a troubled, complex, and crisis-ridden context has also led to a stream of advice that focuses on the very makeup of the leadership role. Some sources (Eaton 1988; Green 1988a; Kerr 1984; Mayhew 1979) suggest specific principles, styles, and orientations to guide the activities of academic leaders. For example, presidents have been advised to choose their priorities judiciously, to develop a good working relationship with the governing board, to ensure campuswide consultation but to prevent the disruption of vetoes by special interests, to provide full information to important community members but to avoid the interference of those groups, to create an institutional vision and to speak out on important social issues, and, quite simply, to be lucky. On a more personal level, they have been advised to be risk takers and to show a preference for individualism rather than affiliation. Presidents have also been advised to select and appoint other competent leaders, to develop solid understandings of how their institutions work, to study their budgets in search of hidden flexibility, to establish and attend to their own agendas, and to exercise good judgment about what can and cannot work. Leaders need to become skilled at symbolic leadership to bridge campus fragmentation, build coalitions to resolve conflicts and find common ground, and build teams to broaden administrative vision.

While advice for leaders is not lacking, such advice is often contradictory and confusing for two reasons. First, observers often use different conceptual orientations to guide their understandings of leadership and organizational behavior. Second, while all the advice appears sensible, much of it is contradictory. Scholars, observers of leadership, and former and present academic leaders disagree about whether successful leadership requires remaining distant or being intimately involved with constituents, whether it should emphasize the acquisition of resources or focus on academic matters, whether it involves accountability or fostering creativity, or whether it requires setting goals or helping others to achieve their own goals.

This section summarizes and critiques some of the major approaches to the study of leadership. The first part considers theories and models of leadership itself; the second views leadership within the context of theories of organization. Leadership has been studied in business organizations, the military, and governmental agencies, but little attention has been given to leadership in higher education (Vroom 1983). At the same time, the study of leadership in colleges and universities may be more problematic than in other settings because of the dual control systems, conflicts between professional and administrative authority, unclear goals, and other special properties of normative, professional organizations (Baldridge et al. 1978; Birnbaum 1988; Perkins 1973).

Analyses of literally hundreds of studies performed over decades indicate that no traits have proven to be essential for successful leadership.

Theories and Models of Leadership

Research traditions in leadership can be grouped into six major categories. The boundaries of these categories are fluid, and they are neither mutually exclusive nor consistent. They do, however, provide a convenient way of organizing an otherwise overwhelming array of materials. The categories include *trait theories,* which attempt to identify specific personal characteristics that contribute to a person's ability to assume and successfully function in positions of leadership; *power and influence theories,* which consider leadership in terms of the source and amount of power available to leaders and the manner in which leaders exercise that power over followers through either unilateral or reciprocal interactions; *behavioral theories,* which study leadership by examining leaders' patterns of activity, managerial roles, and categories of behavior—that is, by considering what it is that leaders actually *do; contingency theories,* which emphasize the importance of situational factors, such as the nature of the task performed by a group or the nature of the external environment to understand effective leadership; *cultural and symbolic theories,* which study the influence of leaders in maintaining or reinterpreting the system of shared beliefs and values that give meaning to organizational life; and *cognitive theories,* which suggest leadership is a social attribution that permits people to make sense of an equivocal, fluid, and complex world. (See, e.g., Gibb [1968], Hollander [1985], House and Baetz [1979], Vroom [1976], and Yukl [1981] for major summaries of research findings in these various traditions and Bass [1981] for an exhaustive and definitive survey of leadership theory and research that cites and summarizes over 4,500 studies.)

Trait theories

This approach proposes that leaders are persons endowed with specific traits related to their effectiveness that differentiate them from followers. Traits may include physical characteristics (height, appearance, age, energy level), personality (self-esteem, dominance, emotional stability, initiative, persistence), social background (education, socioeconomic status), and ability (general intelligence, verbal fluency, knowledge, originality, social insight, cognitive complexity). It is sometimes assumed that these traits are innate, sometimes that they can be developed. Although some traits (such as assertiveness, decisiveness, dependability, persistence, self-confidence) and some skills (such as verbal fluency, creativity, persuasiveness, tact) appear to be characteristic of successful leaders (Bass 1981), possession of the traits does not guarantee effectiveness, nor does their absence proscribe it. Other situational factors seem to be more critical. Moreover, cause-and-effect relationships are questionable, and measurement is difficult. For example, while self-confident people may become leaders, it is equally plausible that becoming leaders may make people self-confident. Similarly, no valid and reliable "units" exist by which the level of self-confidence can be assessed, and it is not possible to determine how much self-confidence is desirable or the point at which others see it as arrogance. Analyses of literally hundreds of studies performed over decades indicate that no traits have proven to be essential for successful leadership (Bass 1981; Gibb 1968), and trait theories are no longer a major focus of organizational research. A fitting epitaph to this tradition is that "personality traits do not contribute highly to effective leadership performance" (Fiedler and Garcia 1987, p. 21).

Power and influence theories

A second research tradition focuses on how effective leaders use power. Two themes have emerged. The first, identified here as the *social power* approach, considers how leaders influence followers. The second, the *social exchange* approach, emphasizes the reciprocal relationship between leaders and followers through which leaders are themselves influenced as they try to influence others.

Leaders who rely on social power to influence followers by virtue of their offices can be identified as officials. Leaders who influence others solely because of their personalities are called informal leaders, and those who influence through both office and personality can be considered formal leaders. In normative organizations like colleges and universities that rely primarily on symbols rather than coercion or financial remuneration to motivate and coordinate participants, organizational control is usually exercised by formal leaders rather than by officials or informal leaders (Etzioni 1961, 1964). Five bases of social power have been suggested (French and Raven 1968). Leaders can influence others through their offices because of the legitimacy provided by our social and legal systems *(legitimate power)* and through the ability of leaders to provide rewards *(reward power)* and to threaten punishments *(coercive power)*. Leaders can also influence others through their own personalities in two ways—their perceived expertise *(expert power)* and the extent to which others personally identify with and like them *(referent power)*. Summaries of research (Yukl 1981) suggest that the use of personal forms of power such as expert power and referent power should lead to greater satisfaction and performance of followers (and presumably to increased organizational effectiveness as well). Legitimate power appears to be uncorrelated with performance, coercive power is negatively correlated, and the findings on reward power are inconsistent. The research has been based primarily on hierarchical groups, however, and causal relationships are not clear. For example, while it may be that less use of legitimate power and legal authority may increase performance, it may also be true that leaders rely less on legitimate power when groups are performing well.

While social power theories emphasize one-way influence, social exchange theories emphasize two-way mutual influence and reciprocal relationships between leaders who provide needed services to a group in exchange for the group's approval and compliance with the leader's demands (Blau 1964; Homans 1958). Leadership thus is not a unilateral and directive process but a cyclic and "dynamic two-way process in which superiors and subordinates repeatedly interact to build, reaffirm, or alter their relationship" (Zahn and Wolf 1981, p. 26). Leaders accumulate power through their positions and their personalities, but their authority is constrained by followers' expectations (Hollander 1985). In essence, the group agrees to collectively reduce its own autonomy and to accept the authority of the leader in exchange for the rewards and benefits (social approval, financial benefits, competitive advantage) the leader can bring them. Doing so does not mean that followers agree to cede *all* their potential power and influence, and indeed several models of exchange theory suggest that leaders can increase their own power by empowering their subordinates (Kanter 1983). Evidence suggests, for example, that members of a working group who see themselves as influencing their superior are more likely in turn to perceive their superior as influential (that is, as having more power) than are groups whose members feel they have little influence on their superiors (Likert 1961).

Leaders also accumulate power by virtue of their expertise and as they produce and fairly distribute rewards expected by the group. Leadership therefore is related to the expectations of followers. To be successful, leaders must either fulfill these expectations or change them (Blau 1964; Hollander 1964; Price and Garland 1981). The difference between fulfilling or changing expectations is at the heart of the distinction between transactional and transformational leadership (Bass 1985; Bennis and Nanus 1985; Burns 1978).

Burns views transactional leadership as a relationship between leaders and followers based on an exchange of valued things, which could be economic, political, or psychological in nature. From this perspective, leaders and followers are seen as involved in a bargaining process rather than in a relationship with an enduring purpose. The monitors of transactional leadership are modal values like honesty, fairness, and honoring commitments.

Transformational leadership on the other hand goes beyond meeting the basic needs of subordinates. It engages followers in such a way as to raise them to new levels of morality and motivation. Leaders' and followers' purposes become fused under transformational leadership rather than separate but related, as under transactional leadership. Transforming leaders are concerned with end values such as liberty, justice, or equality. Neither transactional nor transformational leadership, says Burns, should be confused with what commonly passes for leadership—"acts of oratory, manipulation, sheer self-advancement, brute coercion...conspicuous position taking without followers or follow-through, posturing on various stages…authoritarianism" (p. 427).

Another view of transformational leadership was developed from interviews held with 90 top leaders, including corporate executives, elected government officials, orchestra conductors, and college presidents (Bennis and Nanus 1985). These leaders employed four strategies: (1) attention through vision (having a clear agenda and being oriented toward results); (2) achieving meaning through communication (interpreting reality to enable coordinated action, with the use of metaphors, images, and models as particularly effective in conveying meaning and explanations); (3) gaining trust through positioning (acquired by demonstrating accountability, predictability, reliability, constancy); and (4) gaining recognition or attention through positive self-regard (with the leader emphasizing his or her own strengths and minimizing weaknesses).

One way to differentiate transactional from transformational leadership is that while the transactional leader accepts the organizational culture as it exists, the transformational leader invents, introduces, and advances new cultural forms (Bass 1985). Three factors associated with transformational leadership are charismatic leadership (see, e.g., House and Baetz 1979, pp. 399-401), individual consideration, and intellectual stimulation. To be a charismatic leader, one must possess certain traits, including self-confidence, self-esteem, and self-determination. Individualized consideration refers to aspects of consultation and participative decision making. In Bass's model, leaders demonstrate this characteristic by being concerned with the development of their subordinates, by delegating challenging work, by maintaining contact with subordinates, by maintaining informal communication channels, by keeping subordinates informed, and by providing mentoring. Intellectual stimulation from the perspective of transformational leadership is seen as the leader's ability to change the way followers perceive, conceptualize, and solve problems. The ability to use images and symbols to project ideas is one way in which leaders provide intellectual stimulation.

Transformational leadership creates "performance beyond expectation" and "induces additional effort by sharply increasing subordinate confidence and by elevating the value of outcomes for the subordinate. This is done by expanding the subordinate's needs, by focusing on transcendental interests, and/or by altering or widening the subordinate's level of needs on Maslow's hierarchy" (Bass 1985, p. 22). Such leadership is more likely to emerge in times of rapid change and distress and in organizations that have unclear goals and structure, well-educated members, and a high level of trust.

Even though transformational leadership may be made possible only in rare circumstances by even rarer individuals, it has captured the interest of organizational scholars. Yet an understanding of transformational leadership is unclear because it has been defined from at least two different perspectives. The classic use of transformational leadership, as proposed by Burns (1978), had "powerful moral connotations" (Gardner 1986a, p. 22). As the term gained in popularity, however, it evolved into a code word for innovative or motivational leadership, and the moral connotation has been lost.

Behavioral theories

The third approach to leadership considers neither leaders' characteristics nor the sources of their power, but rather what leaders actually do (Mintzberg 1973; Sayles 1979). Data are often collected about leaders through use of diaries, observation, activity sampling, self-reporting, questionnaires, or analysis of critical incidents. Early studies analyzed the effects on the group's performance of the leader's behavior associated with different styles of leadership. The concepts of authoritarian, democratic, and laissez-faire leadership (Lippett and White 1958) differentiated leaders based on whether they were directive or participatory, emphasized accomplishing tasks or individual satisfaction, and encouraged or discouraged interpersonal contact. Groups headed by authoritarian leaders produced more work, but they also had lower morale and less satisfaction and were more vulnerable to external disruption and to diminished performance when the leader was removed. The authoritarian-democratic dimension of leadership has four types of relationships in organizations, ranging from exploitative autocratic (called System 1), to benevolent autocratic (System 2), consultative (System 3), and democratic (System 4) (Likert 1967). Productivity was presumed to increase as organizations moved away from Systems 1 and 2 (with top-down communication, centralized control, and lack of influence by subordinates over plans or goals) and toward Systems 3 and 4 (bottom-up communication, decentralized control, high influence by subordinates over plans or goals).

The most influential research in the behavioral tradition was conducted as part of the Ohio State leadership studies. It identified two essential aspects of leadership behavior: "initiating structure" (task oriented) and "consideration" (relationship oriented) (Stogdill and Coons 1957). Task-oriented leaders stress such activities as directing, coordinating, planning, and problem solving. Leaders emphasizing consideration behave in a friendly, considerate, supportive, consultative, and open manner. This research approach suggests that leaders should emphasize accomplishing tasks only in certain circumstances; under different conditions, developing and maintaining the group should be stressed. The problem is finding the right combination of the two, and here the literature on the effect of the leader's behavior on the group's performance or satisfaction is contradictory.

One influential application of this approach is the *Managerial Grid*, a two-dimensional array with two scaled axes (Blake and Mouton 1964). A person's leadership style can be located on the grid by identifying the degree of concern for production (task oriented) on a nine-point scale on one axis and concern for people (relationship oriented) on a nine-point scale on the other axis. Leaders with low scores on both scales, identified on Blake and Mouton's scoring system as (0,0), are completely ineffective and demonstrate no concern either for tasks or relationships; their leadership orientation is considered to be pathological. Those high on one scale but low on the other, for example (9,0) or (0,9), are less effective than they could be because they ignore either important relational or task aspects of organizational functioning. Other leaders balance the two scales by compromising the apparently conflicting demands of relationships and tasks, but the compromise results in outcomes—(5,5)—that merely support the group's satisfactory performance. The most effective and desirable style of leadership is one with high scores on both scales (9,9) that emphasizes both productivity and people. The grid has often been criticized for asserting that one "best way" exists of providing leadership without concern for the particular task, the nature of the environment, or the qualities of the participants.

In addition to studying leaders' initiating or consideration activities, it is possible to identify their behaviors as they play a number of organizational roles. An observation of managers at work, for example, resulted in 10 basic managerial roles categorized in three groups: interpersonal behavior (the roles of figurehead, liaison, leader), information-processing behavior (the roles of monitor, disseminator, spokesman), and decision-making behavior (the roles of entrepreneur, disturbance handler, resource allocator, negotiator) (Mintzberg 1973). Another list of 17 comparable "behavior categories" includes, in addition to those cited by the Ohio State studies and by Mintzberg, such activities as inspiring, setting goals, and clarifying roles (Bass 1981). Another series of essays has continued this tradition by describing leaders' attributes and their uses of power as they perform such tasks of leadership as renewing the organization, motivating others, envisioning goals, affirming values, managing, and representing the group (Gardner 1986a, 1986b, 1986c, 1986d, 1986e, 1987a, 1987b, 1987c, 1988a, 1988b, 1988c).

The usefulness of these theories in helping to define behavior leading to effective leadership is problematic, at least in part because no agreement exists on categories among the many classification systems that have been proposed. All of them assume that leaders are effective when they engage in those activities that are most important for the specific situation, so that effective and ineffective leadership changes as the situation changes. But research on the relationship of the leader's behavior to the group's performance or its satisfaction often gives equivocal results (Korman 1966). Among other things, subordinates' performance may influence the leader's behavior as much as the reverse (Crowe, Bochner, and Clark 1972; Greene 1975, 1979), so that the direction of causality is questionable and the presumed relationship between behavior and effectiveness almost tautological. It is relatively easy to call certain behaviors of leaders "effective" once the desired outcomes are observed but much more difficult to stipulate in advance the behaviors of leaders that will have the desired outcomes.

Contingency theories
The fourth perspective on leadership emphasizes the importance of situational factors, such as the nature of the task performed by a group and the nature of the external environment. The theories assume that different situations require different patterns of traits and behavior for a leader to be effective. Because effective behavior is contingent on the situation,

they are collectively referred to as "contingency theories."

Behavioral theories and contingency theories overlap considerably. Both concur that effective behavior depends on the nature of the situation, with contingency theories tending to emphasize the importance of factors outside the organization, while behavioral theories more frequently focus on internal variables. Different models have proposed that effective leadership depends on factors like the nature of the external environment, the type of task, the personal qualities of the leader, leader-follower relations, maturity of followers, followers' expectations, presence or absence of a crisis, availability of reward systems, clarification of role, or any one of dozens of other factors, depending upon the specific theory (Bass 1981; Yukl 1981). These theories essentially say that no single approach to leadership is the best but at the same time that not all approaches are equally effective. The answer to the question "what is effective leadership?" is "it all depends."

Contingency theories attempt to indicate how the leaders' behavior is shaped and thus constrained by situational factors and unfolding events, including pressures to conform to others' expectations, institutional regulations and routines, orders by superiors, nature of the task, perception of the external environment, feedback about organizational effectiveness, environmental complexity and stability, organizational structure, interdependence of subunits, complexity of tasks, and subordinates' orientation toward goals. Some observers suggest that leaders' behavior may be shaped by their level in the hierarchy (leaders at lower levels have less discretion), the nature of the functions of the organizational unit (production leaders can be more directive than research leaders), characteristics of the task and the technology (leaders of low-complexity tasks can be more authoritarian), size of the organizational unit (leaders of larger units engage in less support behavior), lateral interdependence (leaders of interdependent groups are less responsive to their subordinates), subordinates' competence (effective leaders emphasize performance with weaker subordinates), and presence of a crisis (leaders are expected to act more decisively in crises) (see, e.g., Bass 1985; Mintzberg 1973; Sayles 1979; Yukl 1981).

Several contingency models have become well known. Fiedler's *contingency model* (Fiedler 1967, 1971) suggests that leaders are primarily motivated to be either task or relations oriented. The effectiveness of either orientation depends on the nature of relations between leader and members (supportive or nonsupportive), structure of the task (clear or ambiguous), and positional power (high or low) in specific situations. These three factors combine in various ways to produce situations ranging from those in which leaders have high control (good relations, structured task, and high power) to those of low control (nonsupportive relations, ambiguous task, and low power). Task-motivated leaders will be most effective in situations in which they have either high or low control; relationship-oriented leaders will be most effective when their situational control is moderate. It is therefore misleading to speak of a person as a "good" or "bad" leader, as effectiveness differs between situations depending on the leader's personality and degree of situational control. This theory suggests that the most effective way of improving leadership is not to change a person's style of leadership but to place leaders into positions suitable to their leadership orientation or to have them alter their situations to be consistent with their strengths.

More recently, Fiedler has further developed the contingency model by incorporating into it two factors that have largely been ignored or found to be unrelated to a leader's performance—the leader's intelligence and the leader's competence and experience (Fiedler and Garcia 1987). The new approach, called *cognitive resource theory*, assumes that intelligent and competent leaders make more effective plans and decisions than others and that intelligent and directive leaders should therefore be more effective under low stress than less intelligent ones. If the leader is under high stress, however, the leader's intelligence will be diverted from the problem to the source of the stress, and performance will then be related to the leader's job-relevant experience rather than to intelligence. The relationship of intelligence and experience to the leader's effectiveness therefore depends on several factors, including the level of stress, the degree of group support, the directive or nondirective orientation of the leader, and the leader's emphasis upon task or relationship motivation. Cognitive resource theory also suggests that the relative intellectual abilities of groups and leaders may affect the group's performance. In activities in which the group's abilities are correlated negatively with performance, high-ability leaders may be effective. When both the leader's and the group's abilities are high, however, competition and rivalry between them may inhibit the group's performance.

While Fiedler's contingency model is probably the best known, it is by no means the only contingency approach. The *situational leadership theory*, for example, relates appropriate behavior of leaders to the maturity (motivation to achieve, willingness to take responsibility, and education and/or experience) of followers (Hersey and Blanchard 1977). When subordinates are very immature in relation to the task, the leader should be directive and autocratic in defining subordinates' roles and establishing objectives, standards, and procedures. When subordinates have a moderate amount of maturity, the leader should engage in considerable relationship-oriented behavior and a moderate degree of directing and organizing work. When subordinates are very mature, the leader should delegate responsibility for deciding how the work is done to subordinates and allow them considerable autonomy.

The *path-goal theory* suggests that effective leaders are those who clarify the paths to attaining goals and help subordinates overcome problems, thereby increasing subordinates' satisfaction and productivity (House 1971). Leaders should emphasize initiating or consideration behavior depending on differences in the task, work environment, and characteristics of subordinates. For example, when tasks are ambiguous, leaders should help structure them; when tasks are not ambiguous but are structured, leaders should be considerate and supportive.

The *model of decision participation* relates the leader's effectiveness to the degree to which subordinates are permitted to participate in making decisions (Vroom and Yetton 1973). The model is based on an analysis of how a leader's decision-making behavior affects the quality of the decision and the subordinates' acceptance of the decision. Acceptance of decision is the degree of commitment by subordinates to implement a decision effectively. Quality of decision refers to the objective aspects of a decision that affect the group's performance. Five procedures can be used to make decisions in ways that involve none, some, or all of the leader's immediate subordinates: two varieties of autocratic decision making, two varieties of consultation, and a joint decision-making process by leader and subordinates. The effectiveness of a decision-making procedure depends upon a number of

Subordinates' performance may influence the leader's behavior as much as the reverse, so that the direction of causality is questionable.

aspects of the situation: the importance of the decision's quality and subordinates' acceptance of it, the amount of relevant information possessed by the leader and by subordinates, the likelihood that subordinates will accept an autocratic decision, the likelihood that subordinates will cooperate in trying to make a good decision if allowed to participate, and the amount of disagreement among subordinates on their preferred alternatives.

Depending on the situation, the model provides a set of rules for determining what decision-making procedures the leader should avoid in a given situation because quality of decisions or acceptance of them would be risked. Effective leadership requires determining the appropriate involvement of subordinates in each decision, which depends not only upon the characteristics of the subordinates but also on aspects of the decision-making process itself, such as the degree to which a solution must be acceptable to others, the availability of data, and the sharing of organizational goals. Leaders can learn to recognize these characteristics and to adjust their styles accordingly (Vroom 1976).

The *multiple linkage model of leader effectiveness* suggests that any short-term effect of the leader's behavior on the group's performance is mediated by intervening variables (Yukl 1971, 1981). The variables include characteristics of the group, such as resources and support services, task-role organization, cohesiveness of the group and teamwork, and relations between leader and subordinates, and individual characteristics of subordinates, such as their effort, clarity of roles, and skills. A leader's effectiveness depends on the ability to correct any deficiencies in the intervening variables for the work unit. The extent to which certain intervening variables are important and need improvement and the steps that the leader can take are determined by the situation. "When there are no serious deficiencies in any intervening variables, or leaders cannot correct deficiencies because of situational constraints, short-term leadership behavior will have little impact on subordinate performance" (Yukl 1981, p. 160). The model presumes, however, that over time leaders can act to change some of the situational variables and create a more favorable situation through strategic planning, formation of policy, program development, organizational change, and political activities outside the work of the work unit.

While most contingency theories attempt to describe situations under which task or relationship leadership may improve the group's performance, Kerr and Jermier's *substitutes for hierarchical leadership* examines the nature of situations in which *neither* task nor consideration leadership may have any effect on subordinates' satisfaction, motivation, or performance (Howell, Dorfman, and Kerr 1986; Kerr and Jermier 1978). Some organizations have elements within themselves that substitute for or neutralize leadership. The model distinguishes between two kinds of situational variables: "substitutes" and "neutralizers." *Substitutes* that make behavior of the leader unnecessary and redundant include characteristics of the subordinates, the task, or the organization that ensure subordinates will clearly understand their roles, know how to do their work, be highly motivated to perform effectively, and be satisfied with their jobs. *Neutralizers* include characteristics of the task or the organization that prevent the leader from acting in a specified way or that counteract the effects of leadership.

For example, lack of control over rewards can prevent the leader from using rewards as incentives for exceptional performance, and disinterest on the part of the subordinate for the rewards controlled by the leader counteracts the potential for motivation. Characteristics of subordinates such as training and experience can serve as substitutes and/or neutralizers for instrumental leadership and supportive leadership if subordinates look primarily to similar professionals for approval, recognition, and standards of performance. Various attributes of tasks may serve as substitutes for instrumental leadership (for example, if a task is simple and repetitive or provides internal feedback), and can be substitutes for supportive leadership if the task is interesting and enjoyable.

Organizational characteristics can also serve as substitutes for leadership. Organizational formalization can serve as a substitute for directive behavior. Rules and policies can serve as a neutralizer as well as a substitute if they are so inflexible that the leader cannot make changes to facilitate subordinates' efforts. Cohesion in the work group and limited contact between the leader and subordinates can also act as substitutes or neutralizers.

These elements may "render relationship- and/or task-oriented leadership not only impossible but also unnecessary" (Kerr and Jermier 1978, p. 396). For example, relationship-oriented leaders will find it more difficult to exert influence when organizational participants need independence, have a professional orientation, or are indifferent to organizational rewards; when the task is intrinsically satisfying; when the organization includes closely knit and cohesive work groups; when rewards are outside the leader's control; or when spatial distance exists between the leader and those the leader wishes to influence. Some of these same factors also inhibit the influence of task-oriented leadership over performance. In addition, task-oriented leadership is less effective when participants have special ability, knowledge, experience, or training and when tasks provide their own feedback concerning accomplishment.

While organizational leadership is important, it may be a mistake to believe that all leadership must come from "leaders." In many organizations—and it would seem particularly true in professional organizations—much of the guidance and support may be provided by the participants, the nature of the task, or the characteristics of the organization itself. "To the extent that other potential sources are deficient, the hierarchical superior is clearly in a position to play a dominant role...and formal leadership ought to be important. To the extent that other sources provide structure and stroking in abundance, the hierarchical leader will have little chance to exert downward influence" (Kerr and Jermier 1978, p. 400). Tests of the "substitutes for leadership" model (Howell and Dorfman 1981) have provided mixed support for the construct.

Cultural and symbolic theories
The models described previously all presume to a greater or lesser degree that leaders exist in a world that is essentially certain, rational, and linear. They assume that organizations consist of people, processes, and structures that can be described, analyzed, and made more efficient and effective. Leaders are a central focus of organizational life. Empirical, quantitative research and rational analyses are considered potent tools through which the essential nature of organizational functions can be discovered and organizations thereby improved.

In contrast, cultural perspectives and symbolic approaches represent a paradigmatic shift (Kuhn 1970; Lincoln 1985) in thinking about organizations and leadership. They assume that organizational structures and processes are invented, not discovered. Organizations themselves represent an attempt by humans with limited rational capacities to collectively impose meaning upon an equivocal, fluid, and complex world. The importance of facts, descriptions of events, or cause-and-effect relationships is not their "existence" but their interpretation. These theories propose that leadership functions within complex social systems whose participants attempt to find meaningful patterns in the behaviors of others so that they can develop common understandings about the nature of reality. Within this context, it is as important to study how leaders think and process organizational data (Srivastra and Associates 1983) as it is to look at their behavior.

Cultural and symbolic views of leadership suggest that organizational participants come over time through their interactions to develop and to re-create shared meanings that influence their perceptions and their activities. These shared meanings can be thought of as defining an organization's "culture," that is, the dominant values, norms, philosophy, rules, and climate that reflect basic, unquestioned assumptions that organizational participants have of themselves and of their environment. Culture can be seen in the way language is used, in the way power is distributed and decisions made, and particularly in the symbols, stories, myths, and legends that infuse specific organizations with meaning (Deal and Kennedy 1982; Martin 1982; Selznick 1957; Tierney 1985). Culture can be thought of as the "social or normative glue that holds the organization together. It expresses the values or social ideals and beliefs that organizational members come to share" (Smircich 1983, p. 344).

Some scholars and analysts propose that a major factor in the success of leaders is the degree to which they are able to articulate and influence cultural norms and values. Leaders are expected to mold culture by creating new symbols and myths, developing organizational sagas (Clark 1972; Martin et al. 1983), establishing and reinforcing consistent values, and in other ways transforming the culture of the organization (Deal and Kennedy 1982; Peters and Waterman 1982; Schein 1985), which is believed to lead to increased commitment to the organization, motivation by participants, and organizational excellence. The leader manages culture to suit the strategic ends of the organization. Leadership of this kind can be thought of as "the management of meaning"; people emerge as leaders

> . . . *by virtue of the part they play in the definition of the*
> *situation . . . their role in framing experience in a way that*
> *provides the basis for action, e.g., by mobilizing meaning,*
> *by articulating and defining what has previously remained*
> *implicit or unsaid, by inventing images and meanings that*
> *provide a focus for new attention, and by consolidating,*
> *confronting, or changing prevailing wisdom. . . . [Lead-*
> *ership] involves a complicity or process of negotiation*
> *through which certain individuals, implicitly or explicitly,*
> *surrender their power to define the nature of the experience*
> *to others* (Smircich and Morgan 1982, p. 258).

While leaders can influence culture, however, no consensus
exists that culture can in fact be "managed." Rather than being
something subject to the leader's manipulation, culture may
be thought of as a powerful constraint upon the individual
leader's discretion. Meaning does not normally develop out
of extraordinary or heroic leadership but rather through the
constant activities and interactions of everyday organizational
life. Leaders who do not appreciate and operate within the
cultural expectations of an organization may lose their influence and authority.

Leaders may be able to affect the sentiments and commitments of organizational participants, but they may have little
effect over the tangible outcomes of organizational behavior
(Pfeffer 1981). A longitudinal study of leadership in large corporations found that chief executive officers had little effect
on most performance variables compared to the effects of
time, the nature of the industry, and the characteristics of the
specific company (Lieberson and O'Connor 1972). Similarly,
data analyzing the budgets of large cities over a 17-year period
indicate that most of the yearly variance was accounted for
by the characteristics of the city itself rather than by the mayor
(Salancik and Pfeffer 1977). Analysis of data collected from
colleges and universities over a 10-year period does not reveal
a relationship between changes in presidential leadership
and measures of institutional functioning (Birnbaum 1989a).

Several reasons have been suggested for findings that question the instrumental effectiveness of leaders. For example,
leaders are likely to have been filtered and socialized by
careers that have made them conservative and homogeneous

and to have their discretion restricted by internal constraints and external forces outside their control (Cohen and March 1974; March 1984; Pfeffer 1977, 1981). The meaning of leadership in such situations is unclear. Leaders spend considerable time in ceremonial and symbolic activities that may have little objective relationship to organizational goals (Feldman and March 1981; March 1984; Meyer and Rowan 1983) but that are still important because they symbolically signal that the organization is functioning as its sponsors and supporters believe it should.

Cognitive theories

Cognitive theories of leadership (Cohen and March 1974; McCall and Lombardo 1978; Meindl, Ehrlich, and Dukerich 1985; Sergiovanni and Corbally 1984; Sims, Gioia, and Associates 1986) are closely related to symbolic approaches in that they emphasize leadership as arising from the social cognition of organizations. In many ways, leadership is a social attribution—an explanation used by observers to help them find meanings in unusual organizational occurrences. This explanation is commonly directed toward persons filling roles identified as positions of leadership. "Leaders" may be perceived as causative factors in organizations because of the expectations of followers, because of leaders' salience and prominence, because of the human need to impose order and seek causes for otherwise inexplicable events and outcomes, or because leaders conform to prototypical models of what followers expect leaders to be (Calder 1977; Cronshaw and Lord 1987; Green and Mitchell 1979; McElroy 1982; Phillips and Lord 1981; Weiner 1985).

Leadership is associated with a set of myths reinforcing organizational constructions of meanings that helps participants to believe in the effectiveness of individual control. These myths influence the perceptions of leaders as well as of followers, so that leaders are likely to have exaggerated beliefs in their own efficacy. For example, the confidence that has been found to be a characteristic of leaders may be more perceptual than instrumental. "Experience does seem to result in a feeling of having more control over the situation and probably increases the individual's confidence in approaching [the] task" (Fiedler and Garcia 1987, p. 41).

Cognitive processes of selective attention and judgmental bias enable leaders to take credit for successes and attribute them to internal causes like their ability and effort, while they shift the blame for failures, which they attribute to external causes like luck and difficulty of the task (Bradley 1978; Frieze and Weiner 1971; Salancik and Meindl 1984; Weiner and Kukla 1970).

Cognitive biases (Kahneman, Slovic, and Tversky 1982; Nisbett and Ross 1980) allow followers to "see" evidence of the effects of leadership even when it does not exist. For example, when groups are arbitrarily told that they have been successful at a task, they are more likely to perceive that they have had good leadership than groups arbitrarily told that they have failed, and extreme (good or bad) performance of an organization is likely to lead to a preference to use leadership as an explanation even in the absence of supporting data (Meindl, Ehrlich, and Dukerich 1985; Mitchell, Larson, and Green 1977; Staw 1975). One reason may be that merely focusing someone's attention on a person as the potential cause of an equivocal event will affect the extent to which that person is judged to be the cause (Nisbett and Ross 1980). By creating roles in which leadership is expected, followers construct an attribution that organizational effects are the result of the leader's behavior. Leaders, then, are people believed to have caused events. "Successful leaders...are those who can separate themselves from organizational failures and associate themselves with organizational successes" (Pfeffer 1977, p. 110). Assessments by others of a leader's effectiveness may be related less to the instrumental behavior of the leader and more to perceptions of followers of the degree to which the leader appears to do leaderlike things.

Summary

Trait theories are the most primitive of the theories of leadership in that they reduce the explanation of leadership to individual characteristics. Although scholars of leadership do not discount that many leaders may have certain traits in common, they suggest that a model emphasizing traits is too simple to explain a phenomenon as complex as leadership. Power and influence theories are somewhat related to trait theories in that individual characteristics like charisma, intellect, expertise, and interpersonal skills are seen as contributing to the leader's ability to influence followers. Within this group of theories, the transactional and transformational models have received the greatest attention. The primary distinction between these two approaches is that transactional theory perceives the relationship between leader and followers as one of reciprocity and mutual influence and transformational theory perceives the relationship as initiated and directed by the leader. Additionally, while transactional leaders are seen as maintaining the culture of an organization, transformational leaders are seen as changing it. The transformational model is considerably more appealing than the transactional model because within the latter model the leader's role is seen as managerial and oriented toward maintenance, while in the former it is seen as an agent of change. Transformational leadership in the real world, however, is probably a relatively infrequent occurrence.

Behavioral and contingecy theories are closely related. Both theories suggest that leaders may be either task oriented or relationship oriented, depending on the circumstances under which leadership is being exercised. The main distinction is that behavioral theories emphasize the influence of internal variables (e.g., personal qualities of the leader) and contingency theories emphasize the influence of external variables (e.g., the nature of the task). Within contingency theories, the substitutes for hierarchical leadership appear to be the most nontraditional approach, suggesting that characteristics of followers (e.g., professional autonomy) or the organization (e.g., standard operating procedures) substitute for or neutralize the exercise of formal leadership. This approach is particularly relevant to the understanding of leadership in professional organizations because it allows for the possibility of leadership to emerge from among followers.

While trait, behavioral, and contingency theories describe for the most part leadership under conditions in which roles of leader and follower are clearly distinguished and assume clarity in organizational purpose, cultural and symbolic theories represent a significant departure from traditional approaches. Instead of viewing leadership as an objective act in which leaders influence the activities of followers through the display of specific traits, or power, or behaviors, cultural and symbolic theories view leadership as a subjective act in which leaders elicit followers' commitment by constructing a reality that is congruent with followers' beliefs and that reflects desired ends. These theories place considerable emphasis on the means used by leaders, including communication, the manipulation of symbols and myths, and

Leadership exists to the extent that people believe it does, and that belief depends in part on how participants. . . construct the realities of organizational life and define the role of leaders within them.

the use of language. While cultural and symbolic theories view the leader as inventing reality for his followers, cognitive theories regard leaders as an invention of followers. What matters is perception: If leaders are seen as doing the desired leaderlike things, they will be regarded as effective leaders.

Organizational Theory and Images of Leadership

Our beliefs about leadership have disparate sources, including individual biographies, social histories, works of fiction, political analyses, small-group observations, and the laboratory experiments of social psychologists. Often these concepts are presented without consideration for the differences that environmental, social, and contextual factors may play in defining and understanding leadership; behavior considered to be good leadership in one setting may be seen as disruptive in another. Because no objective criteria exist for assessing the presence, absence, or degree of leadership, leadership is to a great extent in the eye of the beholder. In organizations, too, leadership exists to the extent that people believe it does, and that belief depends in part on how participants, through their interactions, construct the realities of organizational life and define the role of leaders within them.

No right or wrong ways exist to view organizations. A number of different models have been suggested, and each model evokes different images of what leadership is and how it may be appropriately manifested. In the study of organizations, classical management theory was succeeded in turn by Weberian bureaucracy, human relations models, neo-Weberian models emphasizing decision making and conflict, the institutional school focusing on the structure, history, and values of organizations, and contingency models emphasizing either technology or the environment (Kast and Rosenzweig 1973; Perrow 1979). Organizations can be studied as rational, natural, or open systems (Katz and Kahn 1978; Scott 1981) or thought of metaphorically as machines, organisms, brains, cultures, political systems, psychic prisons, processes of flux and transformation, or instruments of domination (Morgan 1986). Others have described them as systems of interpretation that create a shared reality through the continued interactions of participants (Daft and Weick 1984; Weick 1979), as groups molded by environments (Pfeffer and Salancik 1978), and as complex, adaptive, and evolutionary nonlinear systems (De Greene 1982). Each of these models illuminates certain aspects of leadership while ignoring other equally valid aspects. Using any one of these models or metaphors exclusively can lead to either/or thinking, which is a limited and ineffective way of conceptualizing either organizations or leadership. In contrast, views about leadership that incorporate many dimensions of leadership take a both/and approach. By confronting the paradoxes of leadership, they create conflict that allows us to see the phenomenon in new ways. Ineffective leaders focus on only one model; more effective leaders balance two or more of them (Quinn 1988).

One of the most useful organizational typologies from the perspective of leadership is that of Bolman and Deal (1984), who suggest that organizations can be looked at through four different vantage points, or coherent perspectives, which they identify as "frames." The *structural frame* emphasizes formal roles and relationships, the *human resource frame* focuses on the needs of people, the *political frame* considers the conflict over scarce resources, and the *symbolic frame* views organizations as cultures with shared values.

> *Frames are windows on the world. Frames filter out some things while allowing others to pass through easily. Frames help us to order the world and decide what action to take. Every manager uses a personal frame, or image, of organizations to gather information, make judgments, and get things done* (Bolman and Deal 1984, p. 4).

This perspective of the frame is useful for several reasons. It suggests that both leaders and followers with different perspectives will interpret the meaning of leadership differently. And it is consistent with evolving ideas about higher education organizations as they have been portrayed as bureaucracies, collegiums, political systems, and organized anarchies. Examining the organizational theories that lead to different frames and their application to the study of higher education indicates how changing perceptions of organization lead to different expectations of leadership. And finally, it suggests the desirability of developing cognitive complexity among leaders who will have to contend with uncertainty and increasingly turbulent environments:

> *Managers who understand and use only one or two of the frames are like a highly specialized species: They may be*

*well adapted to a very narrow environment but extremely
vulnerable to changes in climate or competition. . . . The
turbulent managerial world of the next few decades will
belong to the managers and the organizations with a more
comprehensive understanding of the phenomena of each
of the four frames* (Bolman and Deal 1984, pp. 278-79).

Structural frame

The structural frame, as exemplified by the work of Max
Weber (1947), considers organizations as hierarchical systems
of roles with fixed divisions of labor characterized by written
rules and promotion based on merit (Etzioni 1964). Different
organizational structures are assumed to be most suitable
to support different activities, and designing an appropriate
structure is seen as essential to maximizing organizational
effectiveness. Although the word "bureaucracy" has come
to have negative connotations over time, it refers merely to
"the type of organization designed to accomplish large-scale
administrative tasks by systematically coordinating the work
of many people" (Blau 1956, p. 14). Bureaucracies are closed
systems pursuing explicit goals (Bolman and Deal 1984),
and when tasks to be performed are "well understood, predictable, routine, and repetitive, a bureaucratic structure is
the most effective" (Perrow 1979, p. 162). The essence of
a structural or bureaucratic view of organizations is rationality:

> *The purely bureaucratic type of administrative organiza-
> tion. . . is. . . the most rational known means of carrying
> out imperative control over human beings. It is superior
> to any other form in precision, in stability, in the stringency
> of its discipline, and in its reliability* (Weber 1947, p. 24).

Bureaucracies have often been criticized as impersonal, unre-
sponsive, and unimaginative, but their countervailing benefits
have tended to go unappreciated. Among other things, they
are efficient, provide fairness and equity, and reduce the discretion that superiors might otherwise have in dealing with
subordinates.

Leaders who adopt the structural frame "control activity
by making decisions, resolving conflicts, solving problems,
evaluating performances and output, and distributing rewards
and penalties" (Bolman and Deal 1984, p. 39). Because
bureaucracies create differences in status between individuals

higher and lower in the organization and people tend to deal with each other in their official capacities, bureaucratic leaders are often seen by subordinates as distant and aloof.

Human resource frame

Whereas the structural frame suggests that people should be changed to meet the needs of organizations, the human resource frame suggests that organizations should be changed to meet the needs of people. Based upon studies of organizations (Likert 1961, 1967; McGregor 1960) as well as studies of small groups (Homans 1950), this approach is based on the belief that people have inherent needs for achievement and creativity. Effective organizations are those that provide opportunities for self-actualization and self-control. McGregor (1960) differentiated the structural from the human resource frame in his characterizations of Theory X (workers are lazy, resist change, and must be led by managers) and Theory Y (workers are inherently motivated and creative, and effective managers are those who structure organizations to use this energy). Rather than emphasizing control and supervision, leaders who adopt the human resource frame give attention to removing organizational constraints on workers and to such self-enhancing processes as increased participation in decision making and job enlargement.

The principle behind the human resource frame is that employee-centered leadership will lead to increased morale, which in turn will lead to increased productivity. Critics of the human relations school argue, however, that "there is little empirical support for the human relations theory or theories, that extensive efforts to find support have resulted in increasing limitations and contingencies, and that the grand schemes such as Likert's appear methodologically unsound and theoretically biased" (Perrow 1979, p. 133).

Political frame

The political frame is marked by five essential characteristics:

1. *Most of the important decisions in organizations involve the allocation of scarce resources.*
2. *Organizations are coalitions [comprised] of a number of individuals and interest groups (for example, hierarchical levels, departments, professional groups, ethnic groups).*

3. *Individuals and interest groups differ in their values, preferences, beliefs, information, and perceptions of reality. Such differences are usually enduring and change slowly if at all.*
4. *Organizational goals and decisions emerge from ongoing processes of bargaining, negotiation, and jockeying for position among individuals and groups.*
5. *Because of scarce resources and enduring differences, power and conflict are essential features of organizational life* (Bolman and Deal 1984, p. 109).

Leaders who use the political frame see organizations as fragmented into special interest groups, each pursuing its own objectives. Because no group is strong enough to impose its will on all others, they form coalitions with other groups that have some commonality in their goals and that will work together to achieve them (Bacharach and Lawler 1980). The political frame also assumes that most participants in a community are apathetic.

Organizational politics involves acquiring, developing, and using power to obtain preferred outcomes in situations in which groups disagree (Pfeffer 1981). The power of a group to obtain outcomes consistent with its own preferences depends upon the value of its contribution to the political community and the extent to which that contribution is available from other sources (Bacharach and Lawler 1980). In higher education settings, for example, departments that acquire highly regarded external resources, such as grants, are more likely to have more influence over institutional budget allocations than are other departments (Hills and Mahoney 1978; Salancik and Pfeffer 1974).

Leaders who adopt a political frame practice the art of the possible. Because organizations consist of different groups with legitimate interests, political leaders try to find solutions to problems in a manner considered acceptable by various constituencies. Because these systems are too complex and fractionated to be coordinated either through their structure or through appeals to common norms, leaders influence outcomes by analyzing the preferences of different groups and designing alternatives that can find common ground between them (Lindblom 1968) and by developing compromises that facilitate the formation of coalitions that support the leaders' interests. Under the political frame, leaders assist the organization to manage its own affairs, assist in the process by which issues are deliberated and judgments are made, and then take actions to implement decisions (Tucker 1981).

Symbolic frame

Through the symbolic frame, organizations are systems of reality invented through the continued interaction of the participants. The symbolic frame reflects a tradition of research that analyzes how organizational decisions are made when rationality is limited, goals are equivocal, and claims on the leaders' attention exceed their cognitive capacities (Cyert and March 1963; March and Olsen 1979; March and Simon 1958). The symbolic frame parallels many of the ideas presented earlier in this section describing cultural, symbolic, and cognitive theories of leadership.

One of the most important organizational presentations from a symbolic and cognitive perspective is Cohen and March's classic work, *Leadership and Ambiguity* (1974). In this work, colleges and universities are described as prototypical "organized anarchies," a term coined to identify organizations with three characteristics: problematic goals, unclear technology, and fluid participation in decision making. Traditional notions of organizational rationality cannot be applied when institutional purposes are vague and often articulated to rationalize previous actions, the reasons that certain educational practices appear to have certain results are not known, and authority structures and participants constantly shift. In the organized anarchy:

> *Teachers decide if, when, and what to teach. Students decide if, when, and what to learn. Legislators and donors decide if, when, and what to support. Neither coordination (except the spontaneous mutual adaptation of decision) nor control [is] practiced. Resources are allocated by whatever process emerges but without explicit accommodation and without explicit reference to some superordinate goals. The "decisions" of the system are a consequence produced by the system but intended by no one and decisively controlled by no one. The anarchy model assumes a loosely connected world, or one that can be treated as loosely connected because it is bountiful, and large resource "buffers" can be established between decisions. It assumes that the statistical properties of a large number of autonomous deci-*

sions are such that they will reliably produce jointly satis-factory states (Cohen and March 1974, pp. 33-34).

Because the organization's goals are ambiguous, decisions are often by-products of unintended and unplanned activity. Traditional models of organization assume that people in designated roles follow rational processes to develop and implement solutions to identified problems. But the model of the organized anarchy suggests instead that problems, solutions, participants, and choice opportunities make up four loosely coupled streams flowing through the organization. When organizational choices must be made, problems, solutions, and participants may become connected to them because they are contemporaneous rather than because of any logical relationship. These connections develop much as if their elements were all thrown into a large container and mixed up, a process referred to as "garbage-can decision making."

Because of cognitive biases and limits to rationality, relationships that may have occurred in the garbage can by chance can be believed to be integrally connected by participants who create their versions of reality through processes of retrospective sense making (Weick 1979). Because the relationships are not necessarily logical, problems are seldom resolved according to traditional ideas of rationality. Instead, decisions are more likely to get made by flight (problems arbitrarily connected to a decision leave when they find some other decision arena more attractive) or oversight (decisions are made quickly before extraneous problems, solutions, or participants—considered by the decision maker to be garbage—prevent action by becoming attached to it).

The effects of autonomous actors, loose coupling of organizational elements (Weick 1976), cognitive biases and limits, and chance severely circumscribe the influence of leaders, leading some observers to say that "the college presidency is an illusion" (Cohen and March 1974, p. 2) that "personif[ies] the organization, its activities, and its outcomes" (Pfeffer and Salancik 1978, p. 16) and whose influence is more symbolic than real. Elaborations of this concept suggest that leaders are important as a class but not as individuals. A comparison of leaders to light bulbs notes that while they are essential providers of the light that enables organizational participants to work together, the differences between leaders are minor and difficult to measure reliably (March 1984). To properly coordinate loosely coupled systems, leaders must emphasize symbolic management and in particular should focus attention on the expression of key system values, while decentralizing everything else (Weick 1982).

Summary
An organizational frame represents a distinctive cognitive lens that influences what leaders see and do. The structural frame, for example, views organizations as mechanistic hierarchies with clearly established lines of authority. The classic school of thought associated with this frame is Weber's bureaucracy. Leaders with a structural frame are likely to emphasize their role in making decisions, analyzing problems, determining alternate solutions, choosing the best, and executing it.

Within the human relations frame, organizations are viewed as collectivities with organizational members as their primary resource. The emphasis is on human needs and how organizations can be tailored to meet them. The school of thought associated with this frame is McGregor's Theory X and Theory Y. Leaders with a human relations frame seek participative, democratic decision making and strive to meet people's needs and help them realize their aspirations.

The political frame sees organizations as formal and informal groups vying for power to control institutional processes and outcomes. Decisions result from bargaining, influencing, and coalition building. Conflict, not salient in the two previous frames, is here a central feature of organizations. Leaders with a political frame are mediators or negotiators between shifting power blocs.

Within the symbolic frame, organizations are viewed as loosely coupled and as having unclear goals. Organizational structures and processes are invented. Leaders who adhere to the symbolic frame are primarily catalysts or facilitators of an ongoing process.

This section examines works on leadership in the literature of higher education from the perspective of theories discussed in the previous section, suggesting implications of these studies for effective leadership in higher education.

Although studies of leadership in higher education have traditionally been atheoretical, a resurgence of theoretical research has occurred in recent years, and several works have attempted to integrate findings in the higher education literature with more general theories of leadership. A review of the strengths and weaknesses of several conceptual approaches to studying leadership in the context of academic organizations, for example, provides a clear and concise summary of the major theories of leadership along with a comprehensive annotated bibliography of works on leadership, corporate management, and higher education administration keyed to each theory (Dill and Fullagar 1987). Another essay emphasizes the role of leaders in organizational improvement and gives considerable attention to characteristics and behaviors of leaders as developed through the Ohio State leadership studies (Fincher 1987), not only recognizing the contingent nature of leadership but also including a critical analysis of several works on the presidency.

The most likely sources of power for academic leaders are expert and referent power rather than legitimate, coercive, or reward power.

Trait Theories

Trait theory continues to be influential in images of effective leadership in higher education, even though it is no longer a major approach to research among organizational theorists. Works concerned primarily with describing successful presidents, with identifying the characteristics to look for in selecting individuals for positions of leadership, or with comparing the characteristics of effective and ineffective leaders are the most likely to reflect a trait approach. Even though trait theory may not necessarily be the authors' primary orientation, the tendency to associate leaders with specific traits is so common that many works on leadership refer to traits or individual qualities (see, e.g., Kerr 1984; Kerr and Gade 1986; Vaughan 1986; Walker 1979).

Successful academic leaders have been described in terms of personal attributes, interpersonal abilities, and technical management skills (Kaplowitz 1986). Personal attributes include humor, courage, judgment, integrity, intelligence, persistence, hard work, vision, and being opportunity conscious; interpersonal abilities include being open, building teams, and being compassionate. Technical management skills include producing results, resolving conflicts, analyzing and evaluating problems, being able to shape the work environment, and being goal oriented (Gilley, Fulmer, and Reithlingshoefer 1986; Vaughan 1986).

A portrait of the effective president suggests the following personal traits:

> . . . *a strong drive for responsibility, vigor, persistence, willingness to take chances, originality, ability to delegate, humor, initiative in social situations, fairness, self-confidence, decisiveness, sense of identity, personal style, capacity to organize, willingness to act or boldness. . .* (Fisher 1984, p. 24).

A belief persists that in selecting candidates for positions of leadership, one should look for individuals who appear to have such characteristics. Most often cited are confidence, courage, fairness, respect for the opinions of others, and sensitivity. Undesirable characteristics include being soft-spoken, insecure, vain, concerned with administrative pomp, and graveness (Eble 1978). The trouble, of course, is that judgments on the presence or absence of these characteristics are highly subjective. No research has shown, for example, that a college president who speaks in an assertive and strong voice will be more effective than a soft-spoken president. One study of presidential effectiveness compares the traits and behaviors of 412 presidents identified as highly effective by their peers with a group of 412 "representative" presidents (Fisher, Tack, and Wheeler 1988). The prototypical effective president was self-described as a "strong risk-taking loner with a dream" who was less likely to form close collegial relationships than typical presidents, worked longer hours, made decisions easily, and confided less frequently in other presidents. Closer examination of the data reveals, however, that effective and representative presidents were probably more alike than different. In four of five leadership factors derived from a factor analysis of survey items (managing style, human relations, image, and social reference), no significant differences were found between the two groups of presidents. Significant differences were found only for the confidence factor, which consisted of items that assessed the extent to which presidents believed they can make a difference in their institutions.

While this study suggests that effective leaders are "loners" who maintain social distance, the findings of another study suggest that successful colleges are headed by presidents who are "people-oriented—caring, supportive, and nurturing" (Gilley, Fulmer, and Reithlingshoefer 1986, p. 115). Similarly, while the former study maintains that effective leaders are risk takers, the other says that successful presidents "work feverishly to minimize risk at every step of the way" (p. 65). These studies' conflicting findings suggest the problems of analyzing the effectiveness of leadership from a trait perspective. Few people exhibit consistent traits under all circumstances, so that both "distance" and "nurturing" may accurately represent effective leadership as manifested in different situations. If this in fact is the case, these studies provide a strong argument for the need to define the effectiveness of leadership in dynamic rather than static terms.

Power and Influence Theories
Power and influence theories fall into two types, those that consider leadership in terms of the influence or effects that leaders may have on their followers (social power theory and transformational leadership theory) and those that consider leadership in terms of mutual influence and reciprocal relationships between leaders and followers (social exchange theory and transactional leadership theory).

Social power theory
From this perspective, effective leaders are those who can use their power to influence the activities of others. Concepts of social power appeared to be an important influence in shaping presidents' implicit theories of leadership in one study (Birnbaum 1989a). When asked to explain what leadership meant to them, most of the presidents participating in an extensive study of institutional leadership provided definitions describing leadership as a one-way process, with the leader's function depicted as getting others to follow or accept their directives. For a small minority, the role of the leader was not to direct the group but to facilitate the emergence of leadership latent within it. Definitions that included elements of other conceptual orientations (trait theories, contingency theories, and symbolic theories) were mentioned infrequently.

The most likely sources of power for academic leaders are expert and referent power rather than legitimate, coercive, or reward powers (see the discussion of power and influence theories in the previous section). It has been proposed that college presidents can exert influence over their campuses through charismatic power, which has been questionably identified as analogous to referent power (Fisher 1984). This particular perspective maintains that academic leaders can cultivate charismatic power by remaining distant or remote from constituents, by attending to their personal appearance and style, and by exhibiting self-confidence. To establish distance and remoteness, presidents are counseled not to establish close relationships with faculty, not to be overly visible, and to emphasize the importance of the trappings of the office as symbols of its elevated state. Style consists of presidential comportment, attitude, speech, dress, mannerisms, appearance, and personal habits. Self-confidence relates to cultivating a style of speaking and walking that conveys a sense of self-assuredness. The concept of charismatic power that has been proposed here appears to be much different from referent power, which traditionally has been defined as the willingness of followers to accept influence by a leader they like and with whom they identify.

Practitioners and scholars tend to question the importance given to charismatic traits as well as whether leaders stand to gain by creating distance between themselves and their constituents. It has been suggested (Keohane 1985) that a leader who is concerned with creating an image of mystery and separateness cannot be effective at building coalitions, a critical part of leadership. High levels of campus discontent have been attributed to leaders who were considered to be too distant from their internal and external constituencies and who tended to take constituents' support for granted or to feel it was not needed (Whetten 1984). Reacting to the current preoccupation with charismatic leadership, a recent commentary published in *The Wall Street Journal* says "leadership is more doing than dash."

It has little to do with "leadership qualities" and even less to do with "charisma". . . . Charisma becomes the undoing of leaders. It makes them inflexible, convinced of their own infallibility, unable to change. This is what happened to

Stalin, Hitler, and Mao, and it is a commonplace in the
study of ancient history that only Alexander the Great's early
death saved him from becoming an ineffectual failure
(Drucker 1988).

Social exchange theory/transactional theory

College and university presidents can accumulate and exert
power by controlling access to information, controlling the
budgetary process, allocating resources to preferred projects,
and assessing major faculty and administrative appointments
(Corson 1960). On college campuses, however, the presence
of other sources of power—the trustees' power to make policy
and the faculty's professional authority—seriously limits the
president's discretionary control of organizational activities.
For this reason, social exchange theory is particularly useful
for examining the principles of shared governance and consultation and the image of the president as first among equals,
which undergirds much of the normative values of academic
organizations.

Transactional theory can be particularly useful for understanding the interactions between leaders and followers. The
idiosyncracy credit (IC) model (Hollander 1987), a major
transactional approach to leadership, is of particular relevance
to the understanding of leaders' influence in academic organizations. This model suggests that followers will accept change
and tolerate a leader's behavior that deviates from their expectations more readily if leaders first engage in actions that will
demonstrate their expertise and conformity to the group's
norms. The IC model, for example, explains why new presidents initially may find it beneficial to concentrate on getting
to know their institutions' history, culture, and key players
before proclaiming changes they plan to introduce. A study
of new presidents suggests that first-time presidents, not want-
ing to appear indecisive, may overlook the potential benefits
of "getting to know" and "becoming known" by the institution. In contrast, experienced presidents, in assuming office
at a new institution, recognized the importance of spending
time learning about the expectations of followers (Bensimon
1987, 1989a).

Two works relate presidential failure and success in
accomplishing change to presidents' initial actions. These
studies show the relevance of concepts underlying the IC
model. For example, a member of a new university admin-

istration attributed the failure to implement radical changes and reforms to the inability of the new president and his academic administrators to build loyalty—and to gain credits—among respected members of the faculty.

We succeeded in infusing new blood. . . but we failed to recirculate the old blood. We lost an opportunity to build loyalty among respected members of the veteran faculty. If veteran faculty members had been made to feel that they, too, had a future in the transformed university, they might have embraced the academic reorganization plan with some enthusiasm. Instead the veteran faculty members were hurt, indignant, and—finally—angry (Bennis 1972, p. 116).

In contrast, another study illustrates that time spent accumulating credits (e.g., fulfilling the expectations of constituents) can lead to positive outcomes (Gilley, Fulmer, and Reithlingshoefer 1986). The authors observed that presidential success was related to gaining acceptance and respect from key constituents through low-key, pleasant, and noncontroversial actions early in the presidential term. In their judgment, change and departure from established patterns were tolerated because "of the safety zone of good will they ha[d] created" (p. 66).

The influence of social exchange theory can also be detected in works that downplay the charismatic and directive role of leaders. These studies portray leaders as coordinators of ongoing activities rather than as architects of bold initiatives. This view of leadership is related to the anarchical (Cohen and March 1974), democratic-political (Walker 1979), atomistic (Kerr and Gade 1986), and cybernetic (Birnbaum 1988) models of university leadership that will be discussed in the next section.

Transformational theory

This perspective suggests that effective leaders create and promote desirable "visions" or images of the institution. Unlike goals, tasks, and agendas, which refer to concrete and instrumental ends to be achieved, vision refers to altered perceptions, attitudes, and commitments. The transforming leader must encourage the college community to accept a vision created by his or her symbolic actions (Green 1988b; Hesburgh 1979).

Transformation implies a "metamorphosis or a substitution of one state or system for another, so that a qualitatively different condition is present" (Cameron and Ulrich 1986, p. 1). Fear that higher education is suffering a crisis in leadership has made calls for transformational leadership a recurrent theme in recent studies. Some suggest it is an "illusion, an omnipotent fantasy" (Bennis 1972, p. 115) for a change-oriented administrator to expect that academic organizations would be receptive to this kind of leadership. In higher education, transformational leadership more appropriately may refer to the inspirational role of the leader. For example, the description of leadership as the "poetic part of the presidency" that "sweeps listeners and participants up into the nobility of intellectual and artistic adventures and the urgency of thinking well and feeling deeply about the critical issues of our time" (Keller 1983, p. 25) is unmistakably transformational in tone, as is the following eloquent and inspiring call:

> . . . in the years ahead, higher education will be sorely tested. If we believe that our institutions have value, we must articulate that value and achieve adequate understanding and support. We must find leaders who are dedicated enough to the purpose of higher education that they will expend themselves, if necessary, for that purpose. . . . The qualities of transforming leadership are those that restore in organizations or society a sense of meaning and purpose and release the powerful capacity humankind has for renewal (Kauffman 1980, pp. 114-15).

A modern example of the transformational leader may be found in Theodore Hesburgh, who has been described as "brilliant, forceful, and charismatic. . . a legend on campus, where stories of students scampering up the fire escape outside his office for a glimpse of the great man are a part of the Notre Dame lore, like winning one for the Gipper" (Ward 1988, pp. 32-33). Images like this one, along with the popular belief that transformational leaders are concerned with "doing the right things" while managers are concerned with "doing things right" (Bennis and Nanus 1985; Cameron and Ulrich 1986), make transformational leadership irresistible to leaders and nonleaders alike.

A five-step agenda derived from an analysis of the qualities possessed by great leaders like Ghandi, Martin Luther King, Jr., and Winston Churchill attempts to put transformational leadership into practical terms (Cameron and Ulrich 1986). The list includes the following steps: (1) create readiness for change by focusing attention on the unsatisfactory aspects of the organization; (2) overcome resistance by using non-threatening approaches to introduce change; (3) articulate a vision by combining rational reasoning and symbolic imagery; (4) generate commitment; and (5) institutionalize commitment. Suggested approaches on how to implement each step came mostly from examples drawn from industry and tested in case studies of two colleges in crisis whose presidents took actions that corresponded to the agenda prescribed for transformational leadership. Of course, while following these steps might result in changes that make the campus more adaptable to the demands of the environment, it might not result in changes in the perceptions, beliefs, and values of campus constituents that are at the core of transformational leadership as initially proposed (Burns 1978).

The nature of colleges and universities appears to make the exercise of transformational leadership extremely difficult except under certain conditions. Three such conditions have been suggested—institutional crisis, institutional size, and institutional quality (Birnbaum 1988). Institutional crisis is likely to encourage transformational leadership because campus members and the external community expect leaders to take strong action. Portrayals of presidents exercising transformational leadership can be found in case-study reports of institutions suffering adversity (see, e.g., Cameron and Ulrich 1986; Chaffee 1984; Clark 1970; Riesman and Fuller 1985). Transformational leadership is also more likely to emerge in small institutions where leaders can exert a great deal of personal influence through their daily interactions with the campus. Leaders in 10 small private liberal arts colleges identified as having high faculty morale displayed characteristics of the transformational orientation (Rice and Austin 1988). These leaders were seen by others as powerful influences in the life of their colleges and were credited with single-handedly turning their institutions around. Institutions that need to be upgraded to achieve comparability with their peers also provide an opportunity for transformational leadership. Such presidents have been described as "pathbreaking leaders" (Kerr and Gade 1986).

Although with few exceptions (see Bass 1985) leaders tend to be considered as being either transactional or transformational, a recent study comparing the initial activities of new presidents in institutions in crisis suggests that leaders who use transactional means (e.g., conforming to organizational culture) may be more successful in attaining transformational effects (e.g., improving the organizational culture) than leaders whose behavior reflects the pure form (one-way approach) of transformational leadership (Bensimon 1989c). Even in institutions in distress, a leadership approach that conforms to the group's norms while also seeking to improve them may be of greater benefit than heroic attempts at redesigning an institution.

Leaders who use transactional means may be more successful in attaining trans-formational effects than leaders whose behavior reflects the pure form of trans-formational leadership.

Behavioral Theories
Behavior of the leader
These theories examine whether the leader is task (initiating structure) or people (consideration) oriented or both. Blake and Mouton (1964) adapted their managerial grid into an academic grid and applied it to higher education. Their model suggests five styles of academic administration (Blake, Mouton, and Williams 1981): caretaker, authority-obedience, comfortable-pleasant, constituency-centered, and team. The optimum style is identified as team administration, which is characteristic of leaders who scored high on both concern for institutional performance and concern for people on their grid.

Some limited empirical tests of this theory have been performed. A study of department chairs found that those judged as effective by the faculty scored high both in initiating structure (task) and consideration of people (Knight and Holen 1985). On the other hand, a case study of a single institution reports that departments with high faculty morale had chairs who scored high on measures of consideration of people and participative leadership style but not in initiating structure (Madron, Craig, and Mendel 1976). The academic grid appears to have found its greatest use as a tool for self-assessment. For example, the grid was adapted into a questionnaire to assist department chairs in determining their personal styles of leadership (Tucker 1981).

Presidents' perceptions of the similarity of their role to other leadership roles were used to describe two types of presidents—mediative and authoritative, which are roughly comparable to emphasizing consideration of people and initiating structure (task), respectively (Cohen and March 1974). Mediative presidents tended to define their roles in terms of constituencies, while authoritative presidents appeared to be more directive. Additionally, mediative presidents were more likely to measure their success on the basis of faculty respect, while authoritative presidents were more likely to base it on the quality of educational programs.

Administrative styles based on the self-reported behaviors of presidents were found to be related to faculty and student outcomes in 49 small private liberal arts colleges (Astin and Scherrei 1980). These findings, however, may be influenced by the size of the institutions.

Managerial roles

A comprehensive essay (Dill 1984) reviews the literature on administrative behavior in higher education, employing the behavioral framework developed by Mintzberg (1973). The findings (p. 91) suggest that like managers in other settings, senior administrators in higher education:

- Perform a great variety of work at a continuous pace;
- Carry out activities characterized by variety, fragmentation, and brevity;
- Prefer issues that are current, specific, and ad hoc;
- Demonstrate preference for verbal media (telephone calls, meetings, brief discussions); and
- Develop informal information systems.

Although academic leaders are likely to learn from their actions, almost no attention has been given to what leaders learn on the job. A qualitative study based on interviews with 32 presidents reports that what presidents learn from their actions varies, depending on whether they feel the action they took was wrong (substantive error) or whether they feel the action was justified but the process used (process error) was inappropriate (Neumann 1988). New presidents who made substantive errors learned how to sense situational differences that called for diverse (and new) responses, they began to identify new behaviors that were more appropriate to their new settings, and they gave up the behaviors that worked in their old settings but appeared to be dysfunctional in their new ones. From process errors, presidents tended to learn the degree of influence organizational members have on what presidents can accomplish. Some presidents also made action errors, which consisted of taking action when none should have been taken. From these errors, presidents gained respect for personal and organizational limitations.

Contingency Theories
From this perspective, effective leadership requires adapting one's style of leadership to situational factors. Applying four contingency theories to higher education, Vroom (1983) found that if used to determine the kind of leader best suited to chair academic departments, each would prescribe a different type of leader. Situational variables in Fiedler's contingency model and in House's path-goal theory prescribe a task-oriented leader who would do whatever is necessary to drive the group to complete a job. In contrast, Hersey and Blanchard's life-cycle theory and the Vroom-Yetton decision process theory identify individuals with a delegating and participative style of leadership. The contradictory prescriptions may be the result of their development in organizational settings with clearly delineated superior and subordinate roles. Thus, they may have limited applicability to the study of leadership in higher education. The Vroom-Yetton model appears to be better suited to higher education organizations, because it uses multiple criteria to determine participative or autocratic decision making (Floyd 1985).

Although the observation that "a president may be egalitarian one day and authoritarian the next" (Gilley, Fulmer, and Reithlingshoefer 1986, p. 66) is commonplace, little systematic application of contingency theory has occurred to determine under what conditions alternative forms of leadership should be displayed. Generally, contingency theories have found their greatest applicability in the study of leadership in academic departments, probably because decision making at this level is less equivocal than at higher levels of the academic organization. An application of the Vroom-Yetton model to the study of decision making among department chairs concludes that they frequently chose autocratic styles of decision making in situations where a consultative style would have increased the likelihood of the faculty's acceptance of the decision (Taylor 1982). Hersey and Blanchard's theory was used to develop a questionnaire that would help department chairs determine departmental level of maturity and select a corresponding style of leadership (Tucker 1981). An analysis of studies on the behavior of leaders (Dill 1984) suggests that "when given a choice of leader roles, faculty members consistently preferred the leader as a...'facilitator' or one who smoothed out problems and sought to provide the resources necessary for the research activities of faculty members" (p. 79).

Kerr and Jermier's theory of substitutes for hierarchical leadership may be highly relevant for academic organizations. Despite being one of the few contingency theories in which leadership is not seen as residing solely with the official leader, it has received little attention in the study of academic leadership. If leadership in higher education were to be viewed from this perspective, one could conclude that directive leadership may not be effective because characteristics of academic organizations (such as faculty autonomy and a reward structure that is academic-discipline- and peer-based) substitute for or neutralize the influence of leaders (Birnbaum 1989a). Similarly, a consideration of the influence of administrators on the faculty's motivation asks, "What are university administrators to do in the face of so many 'substitutes' for their leadership?" (Staw 1983, p. 312). Because alternatives such as stressing local (e.g., primary identification is with the institution) rather than professional orientation (e.g., primary identification is with the academic discipline) or reducing self-governance and self-motivation are not in the best interests of the university, it may be more fruitful for administrators to assume the role of facilitator than controller.

Cultural and Symbolic Theories

Occasionally effective leaders give symbolic meaning to events that others may see as perplexing, senseless, or chaotic. They do so by focusing attention on aspects of college life that are both familiar and meaningful to the college community. Cultural and symbolic approaches to studying leadership appear in works on organizations as cultural systems (Chaffee and Tierney 1988; Kuh and Whitt 1988). Understanding colleges and universities as cultures was originally introduced in a now-classic case study of Reed, Swarthmore, and Antioch (Clark 1970, 1972). This study suggests that leaders may play an important role in creating and maintaining institutional sagas. The role of academic leaders in the preservation of academic culture may be even more critical today than in the past, because increased specialization, professionalization, and complexity have weakened the values and beliefs that provided institutions with a common sense of purpose, commitment, and order (Dill 1982). Although leaders may not be able to change culture through management, their attention to social integration and symbolic events may enable them to sustain and strengthen the culture that already exists (Dill 1982).

Cultural and symbolic perspectives on leadership have figured prominently in a small handful of recent works that examine the actions of leaders and their effects on campus during times of financial decline. A recent study suggests that college presidents who are sensitive to the faculty's interpretation of financial stress are more likely to elicit the faculty's support for their own leadership (Neumann 1989a). One of the most important contributions to the understanding of leadership from a cultural perspective is the work on the role of substantive and symbolic actions in successful turnaround situations (Chaffee 1984, 1985a, 1985b). The examination of managerial techniques of presidents in institutions suffering financial decline discloses three alternative strategic approaches—linear, adaptive, and interpretive. Linear strategists were concerned with achieving goals. Adaptive strategists were concerned with aligning the organization with the environment, for example, by changing the organizational orientation to meet current demands and thus to ensure the continued flow of resources. Interpretive strategists reflected the cultural/symbolic perspective in that they were concerned with how people saw, understood, and felt about their lives. Interpretive leaders believed that effective action involves shaping the values, symbols, and emotions that influence the behaviors of individuals. The use of interpretive strategy in combination with adaptive strategy was considerably more effective in turning institutions around than the use of adaptive strategy alone (Chaffee 1984). Presidents who employed interpretive strategies were careful to protect the essential character of their institutions and to refrain from actions and commitments that compromise or disrupt the institution's self-identity and sense of integrity by only introducing new programs that were outgrowths of the old ones. For example, they reaffirmed the existing institutional mission and did not attempt to pursue programmatic thrusts that were outside the expertise of the faculty.

Strategies of change that make sense to institutional members and that therefore are likely to elicit acceptance and support may depend upon leaders' understanding an organization from cultural perspectives. To do so, leaders may be required to act as anthropologists uncovering the organizational culture by seeking to identify metaphors embedded in the language of the college community (Corbally 1984; Deshler 1985; Peck 1983; Tierney 1988). Frameworks for organizational cultures suggest that leaders can begin to understand their institutional cultures by identifying internal contradictions or incongruities between values and structure, by developing a comparative awareness, by clarifying the identity of the institution, by communicating so as "to say the right things and to say things right," and by acting on multiple and changing fronts (Chaffee and Tierney 1988, pp. 185-91).

Leaders should pose organizational questions to help them identify characteristics of the organizational environment, the influence of institutional mission on decision making, processes of socialization, the uses of information, the approaches used to make decisions, and constituents' expectations of leaders (Tierney 1988). Researchers also can gain insights into leadership by examining the symbols embedded in the language of leaders. A study of 32 presidents reveals that they used six categories of symbols—metaphorical, physical, communicative, structural, personification, and ideational—when they talked about their leadership role. Understanding the use of symbolism can help academic leaders to become more consistent by sensitizing them to contradictions between the symbols they use and the behaviors they exhibit on their campuses. Leaders may become more effective by using symbols that are consistent with the institution's culture (Tierney 1989).

The "techniques of managing meaning and social integration are the undiscussed skills of academic management" (Dill 1982, p. 304). For example, it has been suggested that leaders in community colleges have consistently failed to interpret and articulate their missions and to create positive images among their publics (Vaughan 1986). While it is clear that cultural and symbolic leadership skills are becoming increasingly important to presidents, scholars still have much to learn about the characteristics of these skills and effective ways of teaching them to present and aspiring leaders (Green 1988b). A recent examination of colleges and universities from a cultural perspective provides administrators with the following insights: Senior faculty or other core groups of institutional leaders provide continuity and maintain a cohesive institutional culture; institutional policies and practices are driven and bound by culture; culture-driven policies and practices may denigrate the integrity and worth of certain groups; institutional culture is difficult to modify intentionally; and organizational size and complexity work against distinctive patterns of values and assumptions (Kuh and Whitt 1988, p. vi).

Cognitive Theories

Cognitive theories have important implications for perceptions of leaders' effectiveness. In many situations, presidential leadership may not have measurable outcomes other than social attribution—or the tendency of campus constituents to assign to a president the credit or blame for unusual institutional outcomes. From this perspective, leaders are individuals believed by followers to have caused events (Birnbaum 1989b). Leaders themselves, in the absence of clear indicators, are subject to cognitive bias that can lead them to make predictable errors of judgment (Birnbaum 1987) and to overestimate their effectiveness in campus improvements (Birnbaum 1986).

Summary

Trait theories and power and influence theories appear to be particularly influential in works on leadership in higher education. Several of the works reviewed tend to relate effectiveness of leaders to individual characteristics, although not necessarily the same ones. For example, while some consider "being distant" as a desirable characteristic, others propose that "being nurturing" is more important.

Even though exchange theories are more relevant to the understanding of leadership in academic organizations, works that consider leadership from the perspective of power and influence theories tend to emphasize one-way, leader-initiated and leader-directed approaches. Transformational theory, in particular, has received considerable attention, while transactional theory has for the most part been ignored.

Behavioral and contingency theories may have limited application in higher education because these theories focus their attention on the relationship between superior and subordinate roles. Within the category of behavioral theories, the most promising approach may be in the study of administrative behavior, particularly as a way of understanding how leaders learn from their actions and mistakes. Examining how leaders learn from a behavioral perspective may provide new directions and ideas for the design of training programs for academic leaders.

Within the category of contingency theories, Kerr and Jermier's theory of substitutes for hierarchical leadership may be of greatest use, even though it has been almost totally overlooked by scholars of academic leadership.

Although cultural and symbolic perspectives on leadership were first suggested in the early 1970s in Burton Clark's case study of Reed, Swarthmore, and Antioch, only recently has this view of leadership attracted serious attention. Cultural and symbolic perspectives have been shown to be especially useful for understanding the internal dynamics of institutions in financial crisis, particularly in differentiating the strategies leaders use to cope with financial stress and to communicate with constituents. Cognitive theories offer a promising new way of studying leadership, but their use in higher education to date has been limited.

This section examines works on leadership in higher education through the lenses of the four organizational frames introduced in the second section. The first part examines works on leadership in higher education according to their dominant organizational frame; the second examines more recent works that have attempted to examine leadership by integrating two or more of the organizational frames.

The works selected for discussion belong to the general body of literature on leadership in higher education; however, special attention has been given to those works that have been influential in illuminating the theory and practice of leadership and administration in colleges and universities. As in the previous section, the assignation of a particular work to an organizational frame was more likely to be based on its implicit rather than its explicit conceptual orientation.

The University as Bureaucracy (The Structural Frame)

According to the structural frame, the essence of bureaucratic leadership is making decisions and designing systems of control and coordination that direct the work of others and verify their compliance with directives. Because bureaucracies are ultimately centralized systems, the bureaucratic leader has final authority and therefore may be cast as a larger-than-life, or heroic, leader. "Much of the organization's power is held by the hero, and great expectations are raised because people trust him to solve problems and fend off threats from the environment" (Baldridge et al. 1978, p. 44). Bureaucratic leaders have been thought of as heroic in that their position at the top of a presumably competence-based hierarchy suggests that they have knowledge and power well beyond the range of the average person. (This perspective is different from the culturally inspired concept of the leader as hero, which refers to the symbolic rather than to the instrumental effects of leadership. Cultural heros come over time to be thought of as the embodiment of institutional purpose, and their exploits are celebrated through organizational myth and legend.)

From the bureaucratic perspective, the president of a college or university is seen as the center of power, responsible for the welfare and outcomes of the institution (Kerr and Gade 1986). The heroic image of leaders in higher education can be found in references to great presidential figures of the past (see, e.g., Kerr and Gade 1986) as well as in current works that idealize the position (see, e.g., Fisher 1984; Fisher,

Community college presidents... gave greater importance to attributes associated with the heroic image of bureaucratic leadership, such as integrity, good judgment, and courage, than to attributes associated with the symbolic frame, such as tolerance for ambiguity and curiosity.

Tack, and Wheeler 1988). The concept of heroic leadership can also be found in presidents' perceptions that they are more effective than average—and considerably more effective than their predecessors—and that under their administration it has been possible to make major improvements on campus (Birnbaum 1986).

The influence of the bureaucratic perspective is most apparent in rational interpretations of the leader's administrative and managerial role and the skills necessary to perform the role. Colleges and universities have many bureaucratic properties, because the same processes that create bureaucracies in other settings do so in higher education as well (Blau 1973; Stroup 1966). The classic work representative of this frame suggests it is the responsibility of the leader to "synchronize" the organization so that all its parts are working effectively and in harmony. The leader's role is to guard against disruption by anticipating and eliminating potential sources of conflict (Stroup 1966). Qualities and skills commonly associated with this perspective include being decisive, being results oriented, having the ability to plan comprehensively, managing by objectives, and being a rational problem solver (Baldridge et al. 1977, 1978; Benezet, Katz, and Magnusson 1981).

The bureaucratic perspective on leadership in higher education can be found in works that focus on administrative and managerial techniques. Such works provide extensive practical advice in the art and science of administration, including how to deal with day-to-day tasks, the appropriate ways of working and communicating with faculty and students, how to use time efficiently, methods of getting the most from people, and how to exercise authority diplomatically (see, e.g., Eble 1978). Such works tend to provide advice that stresses rational administrative procedures. For example, administrative decision making has been described as consisting of a series of sequential steps in which leaders:

1. *Identify problems, analyze them, and decide in what order they should be approached.*
2. *Develop a program of solutions to these problems individually and jointly.*
3. *Organize support for individual parts of this program in proper order and for the total program.*
4. *Get the human and financial resources necessary to carry out the program.*

5. *Take administrative action to effectuate the programs*
   (Kerr and Gade 1986, p. 55).

The rational side of administration is also evident in several recommendations stressing the need for forecasting, planning, and institutional research during times of decline (Baldridge et al. 1978).

Under the structural or bureaucratic paradigms, effective leaders apply rational calculations to most effectively relate resources to desired outcomes. Administrative leaders are seen as establishing and accomplishing instrumental goals, acquiring and maneuvering the resources that will effectuate them, designing adequate organizational structures and staffing them with qualified personnel, engaging in informational and analytical activities before deciding the best means for accomplishing the goals, and evaluating activities to assess compliance with goals (Balderston 1978; Dressel 1981; Richman and Farmer 1976). From this perspective, effective presidents are the "masters of the enterprise over which they preside" (Mayhew 1979, p. 82). They show their control by appointing strong individuals to chief administrative offices and being willing to remove people from office, by devoting time to the details of administration and management, by having a high level of understanding for finances, by establishing their own agendas and priorities, and by valuing the faculty without succumbing to what presidents may view as improper intrusions in institutional governance.

While rational approaches figure prominently in the literature on higher education leadership and administration, the concept of bureaucracy conjures up negative images in higher education. Leaders labeled bureaucratic tend to be seen as hierarchical and authoritarian, if not autocratic. They may be seen as having a "muscle view of administration" (Walker 1979, p. 5). A study of 40 small liberal arts colleges reports that presidents who were classified as bureaucratic received negative judgments from campus constituents, both in terms of their human relations skills and administrative skills. Faculty and their fellow administrators perceived them as remote, ineffective, and inefficient. Although bureaucratic leaders would appear to emphasize efficiency, students on their campuses were found to be dissatisfied with basic services, such as registration processes, financial aid, and the quality of housing. Additionally, the administrative teams of

bureaucratic presidents, rather than displaying alternative complementary styles (e.g., collegial), were found to function in a hierarchical fashion, both in the way they communicated and interacted with the president and with their own subordinates (Astin and Scherrei 1980).

A study of the relative influence of administrators and faculty on colleges and universities reveals a high level of bureaucratic control in private, less selective, liberal arts colleges and in community colleges. In these institutions, faculty senates were nonexistent or were dominated by administrators (Baldridge et al. 1978). Bureaucratic leadership has been associated with administrative dominance over decision making (Baldridge et al. 1978; Bensimon 1984; Reyes and Twombly 1987; Richardson 1975; Richardson and Rhodes 1983). The findings reported in a recent study of community college presidents show they gave greater importance to attributes associated with the heroic image of bureaucratic leadership, such as integrity, good judgment, and courage, than to attributes associated with the symbolic frame, such as tolerance for ambiguity and curiosity. And rational skills, such as producing results and defining problems and solutions, were rated higher in importance than collegial skills, such as motivating others, developing collegial relations with faculty, and being a team member (Vaughan 1986).

The University as Collegium (The Human Resource Frame)

Within higher education, the human resource orientation is best exemplified by considering the institution (or at least the faculty of the institution) as a collegium, a community of equals, or a community of scholars (Goodman 1962; Millett 1962). In a collegium, where differences in status are deemphasized, people interact as equals in a system that stresses consensus, shared power and participation in governance, and common commitments and aspirations. Behavior is controlled primarily through the group's norms (Homans 1950, 1961) and through acceptance of professional rather than legal authority (Etzioni 1964). Leaders in collegial systems are selected by their peers for limited terms and are considered "first among equals" as they serve the interests of the group members. Rather than issue orders, they try to mold consensus and to create the conditions under which the group will discipline itself by appealing to the group's norms and values. Leaders are more servants of the group than masters, and they are expected to listen, to persuade, to leave themselves open to influence, and to share the burden of decision making.

From this perspective, presidents are viewed as the center of influence (Kerr and Gade 1986) and as responsible for defining and articulating the common good (Millett 1974). While the skills seen as important for a bureaucratic leader connote attributes related to "getting results," leaders in collegial systems rise to power because others see them as exemplifying the group's aspirations and accomplishments to a high degree (Homans 1950). Characteristics seen as essential for the collegial leader are modesty, perceiving the unspoken needs of individuals and goals of groups, placing institutional interests ahead of one's own, being able to listen, facilitating rather than commanding group processes, and influencing rather than dominating through persuasion. Leaders gain acceptance, respect, attention, and trust of campus constituents and colleagues by demonstrating professional expertise and interpersonal skills (Baldridge et al. 1977).

While decision making in the collegium may be understood as a rational process similar to that discussed under the bureaucracy, leaders place emphasis on the processes involved in defining priorities, problems, goals, and tasks to which institutional energies and resources will be devoted. Within this perspective, leaders are viewed as less concerned with hierarchical relationships. They believe that the organization's core is not its leadership so much as its membership. The job of leaders is to promote consensus within the community—and especially between administrators and faculty.

Under the human resource or collegial paradigm, effective leaders are those who view themselves as working with respected colleagues. They see talent and expertise diffused throughout the organization and not lodged solely in hierarchical leadership. They believe that it is the responsibility of leaders to discover and elicit such expertise for the good of the community. The leader's job is not to control or to direct but to facilitate and encourage.

While many presidents consider themselves to operate in a collegial mode, campus constituents do not always see them that way (Bensimon 1988). To be an effective collegial leader may require considerable attention to communication processes. From the comparative descriptions of authoritarian and democratic leaders (Powers and Powers 1983), it can be inferred that effective collegial leaders gain authority by demonstrating the ability to orchestrate consultation rather than relying on authoritarian tactics. Collegial leaders do not act alone; they use processes and structures to involve those who will be affected by the decisions made.

The following guidelines have been proposed for academic leaders who want to implement consultative practices: (1) consultation should occur early in the decision-making process; (2) the procedures for consultation should be uniform and fair to all parties; (3) adequate time should be provided for responding to requests for consultation; (4) access to information relevant to the decision should be readily available; (5) the advice rendered must be adequately considered and feedback given; and (6) the decision, when made, should be communicated to the consulting group (Mortimer and McConnell 1978, p. 275). It is generally agreed that consultative and participatory processes are highly desirable in academic organizations; however, it has been noted that if these processes are to be effectively implemented, greater attention must be given to the training of administrators in participatory leadership skills (Floyd 1985).

Collegial leadership tends to be associated with positive campus outcomes. For example, a case study of 10 small independent colleges attributes high faculty morale and satisfaction in part to leaders who were aggressively participatory, empowering, willing to share information, and willing to promote a strong role for faculty leadership (Rice and Austin 1988). Presidents and faculty members may not agree on the proper role of faculty leadership on their campuses, however.

In one study, presidents tended to emphasize the role of faculty leadership in performing and supporting traditional academic activities, while faculty officers emphasized their role in protecting faculty rights and promoting their welfare (Neumann 1987). Additionally, presidents and faculty were more likely to have inconsistent views about the meaning of good faculty leadership in community and state colleges than in universities and independent colleges. In some ways, these findings lend support to the declaration that collegial governance has died, except perhaps in elite liberal arts colleges (Baldridge et al. 1978).

Although the literature on the collegial model includes discussions of the responsibility of the collective faculty to assume a leadership role on campus, limited attention has been given to the roles of individual faculty leaders at the policy-making level. An extensive review of the literature on faculty participation in decision making observes:

> *The higher education literature does not provide any focused coverage of the leadership role played by faculty serving in roles like chair of the campuswide academic senate or chair of a committee directly advisory to a president or academic vice president. Both the interactions between faculty leaders and other faculty participants and the interactions between faculty leaders and administrative leaders should be examined. It is likely that rather major modifications will be necessary to apply generic organization theory to such faculty leadership, which has no direct parallel in business or other organizational settings* (Floyd 1985, p. 68).

Collegial approaches to leadership are not without critics. Some blame the absence of strong leadership on the myths of the collegium, maintaining that "dual leadership does not work" (Keller 1983, p. 35). Studies of public institutions also suggest that a purely collegial approach is not likely to be effective in the majority of these institutions, as it ignores the conflict and adversarial relations that may be characteristic of unionized institutions and fails to take into account the influence of external authorities in institutional affairs (Mortimer and McConnell 1978).

Other critics suggest that faculty and administration consist of two distinct cultures, making a process of developing consensus based on shared values unlikely. Furthermore, invoking "the best interests of the institution" as the evaluative criterion guiding decision making gives the process a sense of rationality, even though it is based on a standard that is undefinable. From this perspective, collegial approaches, such as consultation, can be thought of as myths to make decision making appear rational rather than political (Lunsford 1970).

The University as Political System
(The Political Frame)
The political model as applied to higher education (Baldridge 1971) focuses on processes that commit an organization to specific goals and sets the strategies for reaching those goals.

Because most people most of the time find establishing policy an uninteresting, unrewarding activity, policy making is usually left to administrators. Participation is fluid as people move in and out of the decision-making process. Decisions are made by those who persist, usually by small groups of political elites who govern most major decisions. Conflict is a normal condition of the model; it increases as resources become scarce. The pressures exerted by internal groups can, as well as the activities of external audiences and constituents, severely limit formal authority.

When leadership in higher education is viewed through the political frame, leaders are considered mediators or negotiators between shifting power blocs and as policy makers presiding over a cabinet form of administration. The leader's power is based on the control of information and manipulation of expertise rather than on official position within a hierarchical structure, as in the case of the structural frame, or the respect of colleagues based on professional expertise, as in the case of the human resource frame.

Under the political paradigm, effective leadership is seen as catalytic (Whetten 1984). Catalytic leaders concentrate on building support from constituents, on establishing jointly supported objectives, and on fostering respect among all interest groups. They rely on diplomacy and persuasion; they are willing to compromise on means but unwilling to compromise on ends (Birnbaum 1988). One of the best-known portrayals of the political role characterizes the president as:

> ...*leader, educator, creator, initiator, wielder of power, pump; he is also office holder, caretaker, inheritor, consensus seeker, persuader, bottleneck. But he is mostly a mediator. The first task of the mediator is peace...peace within the student body, the faculty, the trustees; and peace between and among them* (Kerr 1963, p. 36).

A valuable discussion of the role of college presidents from a political perspective, Walker's highly personalized observations about presidential leadership demonstrate a complex understanding of organizations from an open-systems perspective that incorporates both political and symbolic elements of university organization (1979). Consequently, his observations and comments have an interpretive quality that go beyond the mere recollection of anecdotes. In his democratic-political model of leadership, presidents are problem solvers rather than bureaucratic decision makers. The difference is that decision makers see themselves as single-handedly making tough choices, whereas problem solvers see themselves as presiding over a process that involves negotiating, interpreting, and compromising with many powerful individuals over many potentially good solutions. The problem-solving style requires that leaders be open and communicative so that all parties have access to the same information, that they first consult the people closest to the problem, and that they avoid committing themselves irrevocably or too early to a preferred solution that may undermine the emergence of more plausible options. Leaders who adhere to this style should also be sensitive to giving and sharing credit with others, valuing patience, perseverance, criticism, and fairness.

Tactics recommended to academic leaders who wish to be politically effective include giving constituents advance notice of actions they plan to take, being sensitive to timing announcements with the mood of the campus, keeping members of the cabinet informed and enlisting their support, and personally soliciting the support of constituents (Kellerman 1987; Richardson, Blocker, and Bender 1972). During financial crises, a style of leadership that combines political acumen (involving important campus constituencies) and rational management processes (gaining good information) will be more beneficial than resorting to a bureaucratic crisis-centered style of management (McCorkle and Archibald 1982). Scholars, disagree, however, about the benefits of consultative processes during crises (Hammond 1981).

Critics of the political aspects of campus leadership have focused on the president's role in resolving conflicts among power blocs within the university. Power blocs are depicted as a "conspiracy against leadership" (Kerr and Gade 1986, p. 143), and polycentric authority is seen not as a system of checks and balances (Walker 1979) but as a system "organized more to stop things than to get things done" (Kerr and Gade 1986, p. 145). Partial support for this view might be found in the belief that consensus politics is under strain because interest groups or power blocs tend to compete rather than to cooperate, unlike the consultative processes associated with a political style of leadership (Kellerman 1987).

During financial crises, a style of leadership that combines political acumen and rational management processes will be more beneficial than resorting to a bureaucratic crisis-centered style of management.

The University as Organized Anarchy
(The Symbolic Frame)

When leadership in higher education is viewed through the symbolic frame, leaders serve primarily as facilitators of an ongoing process. This perspective, which is influenced by the cognitive approaches to leadership discussed in the second section, emphasizes the effect leaders have on the expressive side rather than on the instrumental side of organizations. They channel the institution's activities in subtle ways. They do not command, but negotiate. They do not plan comprehensively, but try to apply preexisting solutions to problems (Baldridge et al. 1978). An administrative leader might be seen as one who brings about a sense of organizational purpose and orderliness through interpretation, elaboration, and reinforcement of institutional culture.

The symbolic view of organizations challenges two basic beliefs about leadership. One is the belief in the efficacy of leadership, which presumes that leaders have the power and resources to make choices that will affect organizational outcomes. The other is the belief in differential success among leaders, which presumes that individuals possess attributes that determine their success or failure as leaders (March 1982). The symbolic view stresses that administrative discretion is constrained by many factors. It also emphasizes, however, that academic leaders usually have more influence than other organizational participants and that they can use that influence to make marginal changes supporting their own desired outcomes.

Eight tactical rules have been suggested for leadership in the organized anarchy (Cohen and March 1974) and have been elaborated and illustrated with practical problems relevant to the administration of higher education (Birnbaum 1988):

1. *Spend time.* A leader who is well informed about an issue and gives it full and consistent attention is more likely to be in a position to influence outcomes.
2. *Persist.* Initial rejection of an idea, project, or solution should be seen as a temporary condition rather than an irreversible defeat. The longer a leader persists in pushing for something, the more likely it is to get accepted.
3. *Exchange status for substance.* Leaders who can suppress their need for recognition by letting others take the credit

or by sharing credit with others may be more successful in gaining approval for programs they suggest.

4. *Facilitate the opposition's participation.* Sharing problem-solving authority with opponents is likely to diminish their aspirations and discourage expressions of discontent.

5. *Overload the system.* Proposing many new issues and new projects simultaneously may increase the likelihood that some will be accepted without close scrutiny.

6. *Provide garbage cans.* Making a proposal always involves the risk that it will attract other unrelated and unresolved problems. To avoid having one's proposal buried by such "garbage," always try to make "garbage cans" available in the form of alternative forums in which other people's problems can be expressed.

7. *Manage unobtrusively.* Large-scale effects may be more obtainable by making small and unobtrusive changes rather than major changes, which can trigger opposition and alarm among campus constituents.

8. *Interpret history.* Records of meetings, decisions made, and significant campus activities should be prepared long enough after the event so that they can be written to appear consistent with actions seen as desirable in the present.

Because the symbolic perspective on leadership consists of propositions that challenge widely held ideas about leadership, it has attracted a fair amount of criticism. The suggestion that presidents may have only limited effects on organizational outcomes has been interpreted as disparagement of the presidency. Critics have become overly preoccupied with literal interpretations of the conceptual metaphors (e.g., the implications of labeling the university an "organized anarchy" or the comparison of presidents to light bulbs) and the rigor of Cohen and March's research methodology (1974) (see, e.g., Fincher 1987; Millett 1978; Trow 1985). As a consequence, a tendency exists to overlook subtle but very important ideas concerning the meaning of symbolic leadership— for example, that presidents can have an impact on institutional functioning if they pay greater attention to initiating and maintaining structures and processes designed to attend to the expressive side of their institutions than if they become overly preoccupied with imposing rational control in an organizational form that is antagonistic to it.

But even those who criticize the concept of organized anarchy (e.g., Kerr and Gade 1986) appear to accept many of its premises in their alternative model labeled "atomistic decision making in a shared environment." This model assumes that the autonomy enjoyed by individual members of the academic community and the absence of a clear purpose constrain the exercise of leadership. Additionally, the presidency is seen as bound by context so that actions that could result in effective leadership in one setting could lead to failure of leadership in another. In the "atomistic model," presidents act as "the guardians of the community, maintaining it and, when necessary, changing it—a little at a time" (p. 154). The president is not seen as playing an active role in the decisions being made, except perhaps when a serious internal or external threat arises. Within this model, the president needs to be well informed, must be sensitive about any threats, and must be selective about intervention. While the atomistic model of leadership is not linked conceptually to any particular theory of leadership or organizational behavior, the underlying assumptions are substantively similar to those in the organized anarchy model.

Despite the criticisms of organized anarchy:

> . . . *academic management is still highly intuitive, tends to avoid the use of quantitative data or available management technology, and is subject to the political influence of various powerful groups and interests. . . . In short, the garbage can model of decision making and the institutional context of organized anarchy . . . receive much support from the available research on administrative behavior* (Dill 1984, p. 92).

The University as Cybernetic System
While approaches associated with bureaucratic and collegial frames are easily differentiated from one another, more overlap is evident among the collegial, political, and symbolic approaches to leadership. Consultative processes, for example, play an important role in both the collegial and political models, and open communication and unobtrusive management are considered important skills in the political and symbolic models.

While the models may appear to be competing, in many ways they are complementary. Each illuminates certain aspects of organizations and leadership while obscuring others. A fifth model—the university as a cybernetic system—has been proposed as one way to integrate important aspects of bureaucratic, collegial, political, and symbolic concepts into a comprehensive view of how academic institutions work (Birnbaum 1988). Within this model, institutions are seen as controlled in part by negative feedback loops created and reinforced in the institution's (bureaucratic) structure and negative feedback loops created and reinforced in the institution's (collegial) social system. The balance and relative importance of these loops are mediated by systems of (political) power and cultural and cognitive (symbolic) elements unique to the institution. In the cybernetic organization (Steinbruner 1974), institutional performance is continuously assessed by "monitors"—institutional leaders or groups interested in a limited number of specific aspects of organizational functioning. If organizational performance in a monitored area (e.g., minority enrollment, faculty parking) falls below the threshold considered acceptable by a monitor, the monitor is activated to alert others to the "problem" and to press for corrective action.

For the system to work, leaders must know what kind of negative feedback is important, they must appoint capable and responsible "monitors" for outcomes considered by the leader to be important, and they must be sure that the monitors are free to present the negative feedback that is detected. Cybernetic institutions tend to run themselves, and leaders tend to respond to disruptions or to improve activities through subtle interventions rather than engaging in dramatic attempts to radically change institutional functioning. This approach does not mean that leaders are unnecessary to the system or that they have no effect on it but rather that their effectiveness depends on their functioning according to specific cybernetic principles.

The principles of cybernetic administration (Birnbaum 1988; Morgan 1986; Weick 1979) reflect the integration of organizational theory, leadership theory, and higher education:

1. Leaders should "complicate" themselves by learning to look at problems and events through the four different organizational frames and change their behavior to match changing situational demands.
2. Leaders should become more sensitive to the possibility

of unanticipated consequences of their actions. Effective cybernetic leaders are able to define and design problems in a manner that enables them to be addressed by ongoing organizational structures and processes.

3. Presidents should increase reliance on intuition as they gain experience and are able to understand their organization through multiframe perspectives.

4. Leaders should recognize that decision making is not an analytical, sequential process that culminates in a major pronouncement but the incremental effect of many small actions that make some outcomes more likely than others.

5. Presidents should understand the sources of common cognitive errors and develop habits of thought that question the sources of data and their interpretation.

6. Presidents should encourage dissent within their staffs and seek opinions and perspectives that challenge the status quo.

7. Presidents should select personnel who emphasize different values and therefore notice and interpret cues differently from the leader.

8. Presidents should be certain that data are collected that serve as indicators of the issues with which the president is concerned.

9. Presidents should practice openness by sharing information and data widely and by using a variety of forums to communicate formally and informally with campus constituents.

10. Presidents should know and listen to their followers.

11. Presidents should be good bureaucrats by giving attention to the routine tasks of administration that influence the perceptions constituents form about the leader' competence and the institution's quality.

An Integrated Perspective of Leadership in Higher Education

Integrated approaches are becoming more evident at the conceptual (Bess 1988; Chaffee 1988; Childers 1981; Faerman and Quinn 1985; Whetten and Cameron 1985) and applied (Bensimon 1989b; Birnbaum 1988; Neumann 1989b) levels. Combining cybernetic logic with the linear, adaptive, and interpretive models of strategy results in a highly sophisticated and useful analysis of leadership and effectiveness in state systems of higher education (Chaffee 1988). The analysis draws on cybernetic principles to suggest ways in which systems can carry out their responsibilities for monitoring without controlling institutional affairs. Three models of strategy are used to explain the multiple tasks of system leadership—goal achievement, resource acquisition, and constituent satisfaction.

The concept of Janusian thinking (Cameron 1984), which suggests that leaders should value inconsistency and the paradoxical aspects of their institutions, represents another attempt at developing analytical approaches that match the complexity of organizations. The existence of such paradoxes means, for example, that bureaucratic and collegial systems coexist within an institution, that stability and change both may be seen as desirable, and that generalists and specialists may be equally valuable to an institution.

Much of the current research suggests that the effectiveness of leadership may be related to cognitive complexity. More complex leaders may have the flexibility to understand situations through the use of different and competing scenarios and to act in ways that enable them to attend simultaneously to various organizational needs. Ineffectiveness is related to individual rigidity and narrow interpretation of organizational needs (Faerman and Quinn 1985; Whetten and Cameron 1985). Thus, effective leaders are seen as those who can simultaneously attend to the structural, human, political, and symbolic needs of the organization, while ineffective leaders are those who focus their attention on a single aspect of an organization's functioning.

Leaders who incorporate elements of the four organizational models may be more flexible in responding to different administrative tasks because they are able to enact different realities of the organization and provide different interpretations of events. The display of complex understandings through the use of multiple frames or strategies may be particularly important as the environment of colleges and universities becomes more turbulent. Presidents entering office today appear to be more complex than those who began their terms several years ago (Neumann 1989b). The prevalence of adaptive and interpretive strategies among presidents taking office today suggests that the changes that have taken place in the environment demand more complex and varied strategic approaches.

Maintaining a complex approach to administration (e.g., attending to multifaceted organizational processes and outcomes) is of particular importance during periods of declining resources. At such times, administrators need to remember that organizational health depends not only on the acquisition of resources but also on their efforts to involve constituents, to keep them informed, and to solicit their input (Whetten 1984).

Despite the increasing acceptance of the notion that complex leaders are likely to be more effective than those who think and act on every problem using a single perspective, it is unclear the extent to which administrative styles of academic leaders are in fact complex. A study of 32 college and university presidents who identified the organizational frames implicit in their definitions of what constitutes good leadership shows greater use of one (e.g., bureaucratic) and two frames (e.g., collegial and symbolic) rather than three or more (Bensimon 1989b). The results also show that new presidents were likely to define good leadership from a single-frame perspective, while presidents who had been in office for at least five years and new presidents who had held at least one other presidency in the past were found to hold multiframe perspectives almost exclusively. It is possible that the more experienced presidents have assimilated the potential complexities of the role and so can shift among frames with greater ease.

Summary

This section suggests that leadership in academic organizations can be viewed as taking different forms, depending on whether the university is regarded as a bureaucracy, a collegium, a political system, or an organized anarchy.

When the university is seen as a bureaucracy, the emphasis is on the leader's role in making decisions, getting results, and establishing systems of management. When the university is portrayed as a collegium, leadership is seen as participative. The leader strives to meet constituents' needs and help them realize their aspirations, and the emphasis is on the ability to manage processes of consultation and on interpersonal skills. When looking at the university as a political system, leaders are seen as influencing through persuasion and diplomacy and as being open and communicative. The leader is a mediator or negotiator between shifting power blocs. In

the university as organized anarchy, leaders are constrained
by existing organizational structures and processes and may
make modest improvements through subtle actions and the
manipulation of symbols.

Recent work suggests that leaders who incorporate elements of the four models are likely to have more flexible
responses to different administrative tasks because they notice
the multiple realities of an organization and are able to interpret events in a variety of ways. Leaders who can think and
act using more than one organizational model may be able
to fulfill the many, and often conflicting, expectations of their
position more skillfully than leaders who cannot differentiate
among situational requirements. Integrated approaches to
leadership are represented by the cybernetic model and by
strategic approaches that combine linear, adaptive, and interpretive modes of administrative thought and action.

OVERVIEW AND INTEGRATION

Potential users of research on leadership have often criticized conceptual studies of administration as being neither relevant nor particularly instructive. Our review suggests that the application of some theories of leadership (e.g., transactional, symbolic, situational) could provide academic leaders with insights into processes of leadership and organizational functioning that have not been captured in works that treat leadership as a set of personal characteristics or specified behaviors. While conceptual works on leadership may not tell administrators what kind of leaders they are or tell them what to do, they can be useful in helping them understand the limits of leadership, in describing the difference between instrumental and symbolic behavior and the importance of demonstrating both, in recognizing the importance of the common, everyday activities of leaders that go on behind the scenes and prevent things from going wrong, and in appreciating the advantages of seeing and understanding their institutions through many lenses.

As long as leaders look to researchers to identify specific activities that will enable them to be more effective, they are doomed to disappointment.

The apparent lack of connection between leaders' activity and research on leaders is as much the fault of leaders as it is of scholars. As long as leaders look to researchers to identify specific activities that will enable them to be more effective, they are doomed to disappointment. Research can provide only trivial and superficial responses to those who seek specific answers. What scholars have done—and can continue to do—is provide insights that enable administrators and their constituents to make the organizational world they live in more coherent, thereby permitting them to engage in more constructive, sensible, and personally rewarding behavior. Practitioners often lose sight of the significant effects of scholarship, because the best ideas researchers develop are internalized and become part of the way practitioners construct their world. As simple ideas of institutions as machines become replaced by images of colleges and universities as political systems, cultures, even anarchies, the administrative world view is changed in the most profound and fundamental ways.

Even though it is true that a dearth of research exists in the area of administrative leadership, particularly in the study of roles other than the presidency, some promising new trends deserve recognition. First, issues related to organizational culture and symbolic leadership are receiving concerted attention from a small group of scholars. Second, consensus is growing that the complexity of organizations demands greater complexity in research designs. In the past, scholars have been inclined to define and look at leadership phenomena in terms of dichotomous variables (Fincher 1987). Thus, leaders are seen as authoritative or participative, bureaucratic or collegial, transformational or transactional, task- or people-oriented. By applying integrated conceptual frameworks and perspectives, scholars may better capture organizational and administrative complexity that more effectively comprehends the presence and effects of complementary and competing characteristics within a single organization or individual's behavioral repertoire.

Several themes in this report about the study and practice of leadership merit further discussion: the meaning of effective leadership, the concept of cognitive complexity, differences between transactional and transformational leadership, leadership paradigms, gaps in the literature, and new ways of thinking about leadership.

The Effectiveness of Leadership

Every theory of leadership and organizational frame discussed in this monograph holds implications for effective leadership; at its core, each has a picture of what ideal leaders should be like, what they should accomplish, or how they should carry out the role of leadership. Therefore, conceptions of the effectiveness of leadership depend on the theory being used.

A pluralistic culture can have no single acceptable definition of leadership or measure of effectiveness. In higher education, views of effective leadership vary according to constituencies, levels of analysis, and institutional types. When academic leaders want to know how well they are doing, it might be more beneficial to ask themselves how they are viewed by their constituents rather than assessing themselves against an arbitrary standard like charisma, decisiveness, or courage.

Despite the difficulty of measuring effective leadership on the basis of institutional outcomes, theories of leadership and organizational models influenced by the traditional paradigm suggest the critical role leaders play in affecting organizational outcomes. The current dominant view, as captured by reports of prestigious authorities, proclaim that "presidents make a difference" (Kerr 1984). Causal attributions can lead us to believe that because "strong and bold leadership" and purposeful presidential activity have (apparently) resulted in desired changes in some institutions, such leadership is desirable in all institutions. Leaders who have not been successful can therefore be defined as incompetent and organizational behavior that is not rational labeled as pathological. What appears to be missing from the literature, because research designs have precluded it, is an examination of cases in which strong presidential behavior has not led to improved institutional effectiveness or situations in which effectiveness has improved in the apparent absence of heroic executive leadership.

In contrast, theories of leadership and organizational models influenced by the cultural paradigm suggest that the perceived relationship between a leader's acts and organizational outcomes may be a result of cognitive and perceptual filters and biases.

Leadership is the outcome of an attribution process in which observers—in order to achieve a feeling of control over their environment—tend to attribute outcomes to persons rather than to context, and the identification of individuals with leadership positions facilitates this attribution process (Pfeffer 1978, p. 31).

If this is the case, the difference between successful and unsuccessful leaders may be more apparent than real and more frequently based on luck and the exigencies of the environment than on specific behaviors or skills.

By traditional measures of effectiveness, leadership in higher education seems to be in serious trouble. As pointed out earlier, the onus for rescuing higher education from falling into a deeper state of mediocrity has been placed on its leadership. The evidence that certain kinds of leadership have certain organizational effects is equivocal, whether one talks about corporate executives, sports managers, or college presidents. Numerous examples suggest that yesterday's success stories may be today's failures, even though their qualities of leadership remain unchanged.

The answer to the dilemma of effectiveness in leadership does not lie in more and better research methodologies but in the ability to think about leadership differently. In many colleges and universities, the obligation of leadership to "interpret the role and character of the enterprise, to perceive and develop models for thought and behavior, and to find modes of communication that will inculcate general rather than merely partial perspectives" (Selznick 1957, p. 150) may not belong solely to persons filling formal roles as leaders. In large measure, this responsibility may be fulfilled through the socialization of the participants, professional traditions, and institutional histories. Leadership in this sense may be seen as distributed rather than focused, as "a group quality, a set of functions [that] must be carried out by the group" (Gibb 1968, p. 215). Presidents who accept this idea may find social exchange theories to be useful to them in becoming successful leaders and influencing the future success of their institutions.

Cognitive Complexity

The difference between effective and ineffective leaders may be related to cognitive complexity. It has been suggested here that academic organizations have multiple realities and that leaders with the capacity to use multiple lenses are likely to be more effective than those who analyze and act on every problem using a single perspective. If they are to be effective, academic leaders must recognize the interactions between the bureaucratic, collegial, political, and symbolic processes present in all colleges and universities at all times.

The ability to use several frames and switch from one to another may reflect a high level of cognitive differentiation and integration. Leaders who incorporate elements of several organizational perspectives are likely to be more flexible in responding to different administrative tasks because they are able to create alternative organizational realities and provide differing interpretations of events. Less effective leaders are likely to have simpler understandings of their institutions and their roles. Academic leaders are called upon in many situations to function simultaneously as chief administrative officer, as colleague, as symbol, and as public official. Each role may require different—and mutually inconsistent— behaviors, so that actions that are effective in one context may cause difficulty in another. Because of knowledge, skill, or luck, successful presidents have developed complex behavioral repertoires enabling them to balance these roles. Unsuccessful presidents are more likely to emphasize only one— to act as a manager without sensitivity to academic values or to stress institutional culture without attending to the interests of external political audiences, for example.

One of the best ways for leaders to develop complex understandings is to develop awareness of the various theories of leadership and conceptual models of organizations so that they can generate multiple descriptions of situations and multiple approaches to solutions. Using multiple frames means that a college president can disassemble a process, such as budgeting, for example, and use "political jockeying for position, bureaucratic channels for review, and a collegial summary session" (Chaffee 1983, p. 403) while simultaneously engaging in symbolic acts that cause people to modify their perceptions of reality.

Academic leaders can gain more complex understandings in several ways (Birnbaum 1988). They can practice role reversal, a process in which people try to see a situation through the eyes of others. For example, a president might better understand possible faculty reaction to a proposed administrative initiative by playing the role of the faculty senator and responding to the presentation of a colleague playing the president's role. A president could also engage in frame analysis, considering how people who use each of the four frames might interpret an event or proposal. When leaders encounter what they consider to be undesirable behavior in others, they might ask themselves what they are doing that is influencing what is happening. In doing so, presidents might come to understand how they can influence others by changing their own behavior.

As leaders acquire higher levels of responsibility in the organization, the demand to incorporate diverse behavioral repertoires will increase. Research suggests that academic leaders may become more cognitively complex as they become more experienced, either as a result of learning or because the less complex do not remain long in office. Professional development programs for college administrators may need to give more attention to creative ways of developing complex thinking patterns. More attention needs to be given to how leaders learn from their mistakes.

Transformational and Transactional Leadership
Colleges are reportedly desperately seeking leadership. They seek leaders with vision who are not satisfied with the status quo—leaders who are unafraid of change and have the power and wherewithal to transform their organizations.

Even though transformational leadership in higher education enjoys rhetorical support, it is an approach that in many ways may not be compatible with the ethos, values, and organizational features of colleges and universities. Under normal circumstances, the exercise of transformational leadership in colleges and universities would be extremely difficult, and in many cases it could have disastrous consequences for those who dare attempt it.

Within the transformational perspective, leaders are seen as directing and having a personal impact on their followers; they are looked upon as a source of motivation and inspiration. The transformational model of leadership has three underlying assumptions that conflict with normative expectations in higher education and that therefore are likely to make it inappropriate in academic organizations: (1) leadership emanates from a single highly visible individual; (2) followers are motivated by needs for organizational affiliation; and (3) leadership depends on visible and enduring changes. The presence of two forms of authority in academic organizations—administrative and professional—considerably limits presidential authority and hence the opportunity for transformational leadership. Indeed, the principles of shared governance assign considerable authority and discretion over academic decision making to the faculty. While it is true that such principles may not be equally observed in all institutions of higher education, they are clearly influential in establishing expected norms of shared governance. Because colleges and universities constitute professional organizations, "followers" in some institutions are likely to have a stronger identification internally with their academic departments, and externally with their disciplinary bodies, than with the institution that grants their academic appointments. Faculty rewards are largely controlled and handed out by their peers, and motivation for scholarly productivity is more likely to be derived intrinsically than inspired by presidential acts. Finally, transformational leadership depends on radical change; however, no reason exists to believe that the majority of colleges and universities would benefit from or respond positively to such attempts.

In contrast, transactional theory views leadership as a mutual and reciprocal process of social exchange between leaders and their followers. The ability to exercise leadership is seen as highly dependent on the group's willingness to accept the leader. The conceptual foundations of transactional theory appear highly adaptable to those features of academic organizations most likely to obstruct transformational leadership: the concept of governance as a collective process that involves all important campus constituencies, with particular emphasis given to the participation of the faculty; the faculty's discretion in deciding who should teach, who shall be taught, and what should be taught; and the faculty's prerogative to declare no confidence in the president, which often has the same power to dismiss a president as does a vote by the college trustees. In normative organizations, the leader's role is more appropriately seen as servant than as controller.

It would appear that it is good transactional leadership that affects the life of most colleges most of the time. To the extent that failure of a college can be attributed to a failure of leadership, it is usually not the result of a lack of charisma but to lack of basic organizational competence. The rarity of successful transformational leadership makes it all the more noticeable when it is manifest. But because it is so often related to a complex web of situational contingencies, idiosyncratic personalities, and chance events, little likelihood exists that its nature can ever be truly understood or its frequency increased. This situation is not necessarily cause for despair, however; organizations can probably tolerate only a limited level of transformation, and the constant changes of values induced by a succession of transformational leaders would severely threaten both the stability of institutions and the systems of mutual interaction of which they are part.

Transformational theory is seductive, but transactional theory may be potentially more useful as an explanatory tool for the understanding of successful leadership on most campuses. It also provides presidents with a theory of administrative leadership that is sensible without requiring extraordinary characteristics and supernatural powers. Transactional leadership tends to be spurned despite its obvious applicability to higher education, because it is seen as descriptive of a "managerial" rather than a "leadership" profile. Research and commentaries on the presidency suggest that presidents themselves when they speak of their role have adopted a traditional and directive view of leadership, and few appear to focus upon two-way communication, social exchange processes of mutual influence, and facilitating rather than directing the work of highly educated professionals. Good leadership in higher education may not necessarily consist of doing the work of the organization but of helping the organization do its own work by infusing daily behavior with meaning.

Leadership Paradigms

Contemporary research can be juxtaposed to reflect two major paradigms—the traditional, conservative, or "social fact" approach on the one hand, and the cultural, radical, or social definition approach on the other (Peterson 1985). Several current works examined in this report indicate that the understanding of leadership in academic organizations, at least among scholars, may be undergoing a paradigmatic shift, from the rational perspective toward the cultural and symbolic perspectives. Close attention is being given to the manifestation of symbolic leadership, as shown by works concerning the role of college presidents in the management of meaning, the construction of institutional reality, and the interpretation of myths, rituals, and symbols.

The increased reliance on symbolic theory to understand leadership in academic organizations can be attributed to several factors: the popularization of corporate cultures along with the warning that scholarship was neglecting the tools of symbolic management and the use in higher education of research methods that are anthropologically based (i.e., ethnographies, naturalistic studies). Thus, studies are more likely to observe cultural features of organizations and symbolic aspects of management than seen in classic quantitative studies.

Practitioners have not embraced the symbolic view of leadership. With very few exceptions, practical works on leadership written by present and former presidents do not espouse, even implicitly, a symbolic perspective on leadership. By and large these works continue to be guided by traditional conceptions of one-way rational leadership. The image of the leader with which we are presented is of someone in control of the campus, setting goals and priorities, making decisions, and providing direction and a vision of the future.

The symbolic view of leadership may lack supporters among practitioners because it presents the leader in roles that are considerably more modest (and less alluring) than those of heroic or transformational leadership. For adherents

of the "strong and bold" brand of leadership, the symbolic
perspective conjures up images of a leader that lack both
influence and substance. Another unfortunate misperception
is that the concept of symbolic leadership is often thought
of as doing things for their intended effect—dressing for success, walking around campus to appear visible, or holding
ceremonial activities to show off the presidency.

Symbolic theories deserve serious attention because they
present a view of leadership that is highly compatible with
the characteristics of academic organizations. The ambiguity
of purpose, the diffusion of power and authority, and the
absence of clear and measurable outcomes are but a few of
the constraints faced by college presidents. Viewed from a
rational perspective, these constraints make the presidency
appear to be an impossible job. In contrast, presidents who
interpret their role from a symbolic perspective will be less
concerned with leaving an imprint and more concerned with
helping their campuses make sense of an equivocal world.
Such presidents will be more concerned with influencing
perceptual changes than in convincing others of the correct-
ness of their decisions. In an "organized anarchy," symbolic
leadership may in fact be the rational choice.

While the symbolic view is receiving greater scholarly attention, many studies tend to be limited. For the most part, work
on symbolic leadership remains abstract. The need continues
to identify how conceptual terms like the "management of
meaning," "social construction of organizations," or "enact-
ment of the environment" get translated into the routine
administrative practices of colleges and universities.

Thinking about Leadership
Much of good leadership consists of appropriately doing those
things that others expect leaders to do, attending to the routines of institutional life, repairing them as they are buffeted
and challenged by internal and external forces, and maintaining the organizational culture. These behaviors are essential, but usually not heroic. When they are done well, they
often go unnoticed; when they are done poorly, the institution
may suffer and the tenure of the leader may be threatened.

When things appear not to be going well and the cause
is unknown, a natural tendency exists to blame those nom-
inally in charge and to call for "strong" leadership. It is usually
an exercise in rhetoric rather than of organizational analysis.

No evidence exists that assertive and courageous institutional leadership will have the positive effects that its proponents envision. It is true that we can identify a small number of academic leaders whose institutions were significantly altered by their presence, and in some cases those changes may have been caused primarily by the leader's performance. But in others, "leadership" may be just an explanation for events or outcomes that would have inevitably occurred. It has been noted in medicine that about a third of all illnesses are cured without treatment, and it is likely that many organizational problems can be resolved without the leader's intervention. Just as a third of all hospital patients suffer from symptoms caused in whole or in part by their treatment, leaders have to beware of precipitant actions that make things worse rather than better (Birnbaum 1989c).

In colleges and universities, as in other organizations, processes are primarily influenced by routines, organizational history, and the socialization of the participants—factors over which most leaders have little control most of the time. It does not mean that leaders have no influence but rather that they probably have less responsibility for either the institution's failure or success than they—or their followers—might believe. The same factors that limit the influence of leaders may spontaneously correct institutional response if leaders can control their tendency to act prematurely. "It is simply a matter of not upsetting ancient customs and of adjusting them instead to meet new circumstances. Hence, if a prince is just ordinarily industrious, he can always keep his position" (Machiavelli 1977, p. 4). Fortunately, the processes by which leaders in the academy are selected make it likely that they will both understand the customs and be reasonably industrious. The sharing of institutional authority and influence that characterizes the best practices in higher education means that most good leaders are unlikely to leave a major mark on their institutions. But by understanding and using the self-corrective properties of their institutions, they can leave them a little bit better than they found them, and that by itself is a worthy goal (Birnbaum 1989c).

An Agenda for Research on Leadership in Higher Education
A review of works on administrative behavior (Dill 1984) is particularly valuable in identifying gaps in the study of leader-

ship in academic organizations. Dill concluded that studies of administrative behavior in action are seriously lacking. More specifically, within the category of human relations skills, he identified the need for more research on peer-related behavior, particularly in establishing and maintaining communication networks with internal constituents. Resolving conflicts was also identified as an unexplored area for research. Within the category of conceptual skills, almost no research was found on entrepreneurial behavior, particularly on how academic leaders search for problems or opportunities for change, and on introspective behavior, particularly on how academic leaders learn from their actions. Our review tends to indicate that much of the research on administrative leadership continues to overlook these gaps.

Our understanding of leadership is shaped by our research approaches and conceptual lenses. It is important to allow in our work not only for the possibility that in colleges and universities directive leadership under most circumstances may be ineffectual but also that leadership need not come solely from the president. The theories that appear to have a strong influence in the understanding of administrative leadership in higher education discount the emergence of leadership from sources other than the official role of the president. To advance the study of leadership in higher education, it is essential that we use theories that give attention to multiple sources of leadership. Studies examining interactions among administrative leaders and the functioning of administrative teams are practically nonexistent. This omission is serious because organizational success in professional organizations may be related to the "density of administrative competence" (March 1984, p. 29) within the organization or team efforts rather than individual efforts. No attention has been given to faculty senate leadership or to the leadership of faculty unions. This omission is critical, as these officers are likely to influence faculty agendas, to affect campus decision making and communication systems, and to interact and communicate with the president and other leaders more than other faculty.

In addition to social exchange theories, Kerr and Jermier's theory of substitutes for hierarchical leadership, which has been largely ignored in the higher education literature, could provide a useful approach to determining how the characteristics of academic organizations, of academic work, and of key campus constituencies substitute for or neutralize traditional notions of leadership. This theory could also provide a framework for examining various campus leadership roles.

Present-day theories of leadership have been limited by too much reliance on narrowly focused studies, but they can be improved with greater commitment to comprehensive and multivariate studies.

> *Despite the many apparent points of convergence between the trait research, the power research, and the behavior research, few studies include more than one set of variables in the same investigation, and even these studies fall short of the broad perspective required of truly integrative research. To advance the integration of approaches, some studies are needed with a perspective broad enough to encompass leader traits, behavior, influence processes, intervening variables, situational variables, and end-result variables. . . . If some of [the relevant] variables cannot be measured quantitatively, the researcher should at least make an effort to assess qualitatively how they fit into the leadership process* (Yukl 1981, p. 287).

In the descriptions of theories of leadership provided in this monograph, leaders are seen in roles ranging from all-powerful hero to illusion and symbol. Leaders are described in terms of who they are, what they do, how they think, their presumed effects, and how they are seen by others. They are considered as heads of bureaucratic organizations, peer groups, political structures, and systems of myth and metaphor. Probably each major idea about leadership is correct under certain conditions, in certain institutions, at certain times, and with certain groups. A research agenda for leadership in higher education must recognize that leadership, as is the case with other social constructs, is multidimensional and that its definition and interpretation will legitimately differ among different observers with different values whose assessments may be based on conflicting criteria, units of measurement, or time horizons. For this reason, no consensus presently exists—or is even likely to—on a grand unifying theory of academic leadership.

REFERENCES

The Educational Resources Information Center (ERIC) Clearinghouse on Higher Education abstracts and indexes the current literature on higher education for inclusion in ERIC's data base and announcement in ERIC's monthly bibliographic journal, *Resources in Education* (RIE). Most of these publications are available through the ERIC Document Reproduction Service (EDRS). For publications cited in this bibliography that are available from EDRS, ordering number and price code are included. Readers who wish to order a publication should write to the ERIC Document Reproduction Service, 3900 Wheeler Avenue, Alexandria, Virginia 22304. (Phone orders with VISA or MasterCard are taken at 800/227-ERIC or 703/823-0500.) When ordering, please specify the document (ED) number. Documents are available as noted in microfiche (MF) and paper copy (PC). If you have the price code ready when you call EDRS, an exact price can be quoted. The last page of the latest issue of *Resources in Education* also has the current cost, listed by code.

American Association for Higher Education. 1967. *Faculty Participation in Academic Governance.* Washington, D.C.: National Education Association.

American Association of University Professors, American Council on Education, and the Association of Governing Boards of Universities and Colleges. 1984 (orig. pub. 1966). "Joint Statement on Government of Colleges and Universities." Reprinted in *Policy Documents and Reports,* pp. 105–10. Washington, D.C.: AAUP.

Association of American Colleges, Project on Redefining the Meaning and Purpose of Baccalaureate Degrees. 1985. *Integrity in the College Curriculum.* Washington, D.C.: Author.

Astin, A.W., and R.A. Scherrei. 1980. *Maximizing Leadership Effectiveness.* San Francisco: Jossey-Bass.

Bacharach, Samuel B., and Edward J. Lawler. 1980. *Power and Politics in Organizations.* San Francisco: Jossey-Bass.

Balderston, Frederick E. 1978. *Managing Today's University.* San Francisco: Jossey-Bass.

Baldridge, J. Victor. 1971. *Power and Conflict in the University.* New York: John Wiley & Sons.

Baldridge, J. Victor, David V. Curtis, George Ecker, and Gary L. Riley. 1977. "Alternative Models of Governance in Higher Education." In *Governing Academic Organizations: New Problems, New Perspectives,* edited by Gary L. Riley and J. Victor Baldridge. Berkeley: McCutchan.

———. 1978. *Policy Making and Effective Leadership.* San Francisco: Jossey-Bass.

Bass, Bernard M. 1981. *Stodgill's Handbook of Leadership.* New York: Free Press.

———. 1985. *Leadership and Performance beyond Expectation.*

New York: Free Press.

Benezet, Louis T., Joseph Katz, and Frances W. Magnusson. 1981. *Style and Substance: Leadership and the College Presidency.* Washington, D.C.: American Council on Education.

Bennett, William J. 1984. *To Reclaim a Legacy: A Report on the Humanities in Higher Education.* Washington D.C.: National Endowment for the Humanities. ED 247 880. 63 pp. MF–01; PC–03.

Bennis, Warren G. 1972. "Who Sank the Yellow Submarine?" Reprinted in *Governing Academic Organizations: New Problems, New Perspectives,* edited by Gary L. Riley and J. Victor Baldridge, pp. 110–22. Berkeley: McCutchan. Bennis, Warren G., and Burt Nanus. 1985. *Leaders.* New York: Harper & Row.

Bensimon, Estela M. 1984. "Selected Aspects of Governance: An ERIC Review." *Community College Review* 12(2): 54–61.

———. 1987. "The Discovery Stage of Presidential Succession." Paper presented at a national meeting of the Association for the Study of Higher Education, November, Baltimore, Maryland. ED 292 381. 27 pp. MF–01; PC-02.

———. 1988. "Viewing the Presidency: Perceptual Congruence between Presidents and Leaders on Their Campuses." Paper presented at an annual meeting of the American Educational Research Association, April, New Orleans, Louisiana.

———. 1989a. "Five Approaches to Think About: Lessons Learned from Experienced Presidents." In *On Becoming a President: Advice to New College and University CEOs,* edited by E.M. Bensimon, M. Gade, and J. Kauffman. Washington, D.C.: American Association for Higher Education.

———. 1989b. "The Meaning of 'Good Presidential Leadership': A Frame Analysis." *Review of Higher Education* 12: 107–23. ED 292 416. 38 pp. MF–01; PC-02.

———. 1989c. "New Presidents' Initial Actions: Transactional, Transformational, or 'Transvigorational' Leadership." Paper presented at an annual meeting of the American Educational Research Association, March, San Francisco, California.

Bess, James L. 1983. "Maps and Gaps in the Study of College and University Organization." *Review of Higher Education* 6(4): 239–51.

———. 1988. *Collegiality and Bureaucracy in the Modern University: The Influence of Information and Power on Decision-Making Structures.* New York: Teachers College Press.

Biemiller, Lawrence. 15 October 1986. "Timing the Only Surprise as Dartmouth President Quits." *Chronicle of Higher Education.* 33(7): 3.

Birnbaum, Robert. 1986. "Leadership and Learning: The College President as Intuitive Scientist." *Review of Higher Education* 9: 381-95.

————. 1987. "When College Presidents Are Wrong: The Effects of Knowledge Structures and Judgmental Heuristics on Administrative Inferences." College Park: Univ. of Maryland, Natioal Center for Postsecondary Governance and Finance (OP 87:6).

————. 1988. *How Colleges Work: The Cybernetics of Academic Organization and Leadership.* San Francisco: Jossey-Bass.

————. 1989a. "The Implicit Leadership Theories of College and University Presidents." *Review of Higher Education* 12: 125–36. ED 292 408. 28 pp. MF–01; PC–02.

————. 1989b. "Presidential Succession and Institutional Functioning in Higher Education." *Journal of Higher Education* 60(2): 123–35.

————. 1989c. "Responsibility without Authority: The Impossible Job of the College President." In *Higher Education: Handbook of Theory and Research,* vol. 5, edited by John C. Smart. New York: Agathon Press. In press.

Blake, Robert R., and Jane S. Mouton. 1964. *The Managerial Grid.* Houston: Gulf Publishing Co.

Blake, Robert R., Jane S. Mouton, and Martha S. Williams. 1981. *The Academic Administrative Grid.* San Francisco: Jossey-Bass.

Blau, Peter M. 1956. *Bureaucracy in Modern Society.* New York: Random House.

————. 1964. *Exchange and Power in Social Life.* New York: John Wiley & Sons.

————. 1973. *The Organization of Academic Work.* New York: John Wiley & Sons.

Bolman, Lee G., and Terrence E. Deal. 1984. *Modern Approaches to Understanding and Managing Organizations.* San Francisco: Jossey-Bass.

Bradley, Gifford W. 1978. "Self-Serving Biases in the Attribution Process: A Reexamination of the Fact or Fiction Question." *Journal of Personality and Social Psychology* 36(1): 57–71.

Brewster, Kingman, Jr. 1976. "Politics of Academia." In *Power and Authority: Transformation of Campus Governance,* edited by Harold L. Hodgkinson and L. Richard Meeth. San Francisco: Jossey-Bass.

Burns, J. MacGregor. 1978. *Leadership.* New York: Harper & Row.

Calder, Bobby J. 1977. "An Attribution Theory of Leadership." In *New Directions for Organizational Behavior,* edited by Barry M. Staw and Gerald R. Salancik. Chicago: St. Clair Press.

Cameron, Kim S. 1984. "Organizational Adaption and Higher Education." *Journal of Higher Education* 55(2): 122–44.

Cameron, Kim S., and David O. Ulrich. 1986. "Transformational Leadership in Colleges and Universities." In *Higher Education: Handbook of Theory and Research,* vol. 2, edited by John C. Smart. New York: Agathon Press.

Chaffee, Ellen Earle. 1983. "The Role of Rationality in University Budgeting." *Research* 19: 387–406.

———. 1984. "Successful Strategic Management in Small Private Colleges." *Jounal of Higher Education* 55(2): 212–41.

———. 1985a. "The Concept of Strategy: From Business to Higher Education." In *Higher Education: Handbook of Theory and Research,* vol. 1, edited by John C. Smart. New York: Agathon Press.

———. 1985b. "Three Models of Strategy." *Academy of Management Review* 10: 89–98.

———. 1988. "Strategy and Effectiveness in Systems of Higher Education." In *Higher Education: Handbook of Theory and Research,* vol. 5, edited by John C. Smart. New York: Agathon Press.

Chaffee, Ellen Earle, and William G. Tierney. 1988. *Collegiate Culture and Leadership Strategies.* New York: American Council on Education/Macmillan.

Childers, Marie E. 1981. "What Is Political about Bureaucratic-Collegial Decision Making?" *Review of Higher Education* 5: 25–45.

Clark, Burton R. 1970. *The Distinctive College.* Chicago: Aldine.

———. 1972. "The Organizational Saga in Higher Education." *Administrative Science Quarterly* 17: 178–84.

———. 1983. *The Higher Education System: Academic Organization in Cross-National Perspective.* Berkeley: Univ. of California Press.

Cohen, Michael D., and James G. March. 1974. *Leadership and Ambiguity: The American College Presidency.* New York: McGraw-Hill.

Corbally, John E. 1984. "Theory into Practice: Higher Education and the Cultural Perspective." In *Leadership and Organizational Culture,* edited by Thomas J. Sergiovanni and John E. Corbally. Urbana: Univ. of Illinois Press.

Corson, John J. 1960. *Governance of Colleges and Universities.* New York: McGraw-Hill.

Cronshaw, S.F., and Robert G. Lord. 1987. *"Effects of Categorization, Attribution, and Encoding Processes on Leadership Perceptions."* Journal of Applied Psychology 72(1): 97–106.

Crowe, Bruce J., Stephen Bochner, and Alfred W. Clark. 1972. "The Effects of Subordinates' Behavior on Managerial Style." *Human Relations* 25(3): 215–37.

Cyert, Richard M., and James G. March. 1963. *A Behavioral Theory of the Firm.* Englewood Cliffs, N.J.: Prentice-Hall.

Daft, Richard L., and Karl E. Weick. 1984. "Toward a Model of Organizations as Interpretation Systems." *Academy of Management Review* 9(2): 284–95.

Deal, Terrence E., and Allan A. Kennedy. 1982. *Corporate Cultures: The Rights and Rituals of Corporate Life.* Reading, Mass.: Addison-Wesley.

De Greene, Kenyon B. 1982. *The Adaptive Organization: Antici-pation and Management of Crisis.* New York: John Wiley & Sons.

Deshler, David. 1985. "Metaphors and Values in Higher Education." *Academe* 71(6): 22–28.

Dill, David D. 1982. "The Management of Academic Culture: Notes on the Management of Meaning and Social Integration." *Higher Education* 11: 303–20.

————. 1984. "The Nature of Administrative Behavior in Higher Education." *Educational Administration Quarterly* 20(3): 69–99.

Dill, David D., and Patricia K. Fullagar. 1987. "Leadership and Admin-istrative Style." In *Key Resources on Higher Education Governance, Management, and Leadership: A Guide to the Literature,* edited by Marvin W. Peterson and Lisa A. Mets. San Francisco: Jossey-Bass.

Dressel, Paul L. 1981. *Administrative Leadership.* San Francisco: Jossey-Bass.

Drucker, Peter F. 6 January 1988. "Leadership: More Doing than Dash." *The Wall Street Journal.*

Eaton, Judith S. 1988. "Conclusion: Observations and Recommen-dations." In *Colleges of Choice: The Enabling Impact of the Com-munity College,* edited by Judith S. Eaton. New York: American Council on Education/Macmillan.

Eble, Kenneth E. 1978. *The Art of Administration.* San Francisco: Jossey-Bass.

Etzioni, Amitai. 1961. *A Comparative Analysis of Complex Organ-izations.* New York: Free Press of Glencoe.

————. 1964. *A Comparative Analysis of Complex Organizations: On Power, Involvement, and Their Correlates.* New York: Free Press.

Evangelauf, Jean. 21 November 1984. "Presidents Say They're Spend-ing More Time away from Campuses." *Chronicle of Higher Edu-cation* 29(13): 1+.

Faerman, Sue R., and Robert E. Quinn. 1985. "Effectiveness: The Perspective from Organizational Theory." *Review of Higher Edu-cation* 9: 83–100.

Feldman, Martha S., and James G. March. 1981. "Information in Organizations as Signal and Symbol." *Administrative Science Quar-terly* 26: 171–86.

Fiedler, Fred E. 1967. *A Theory of Leadership Effectiveness.* New York: McGraw-Hill.

————. 1971. "Validation and Extension of the Contingency Model of Leadership Effectiveness: A Review of the Empirical Find-ings." *Psychological Bulletin* 76(2): 128–48.

Fiedler, Fred E., and J.E. Garcia. 1987. *New Approaches to Effective Leadership.* New York: John Wiley & Sons.

Fincher, Cameron. 1987. "Administrative Leadership in Higher Education." In *Higher Education: Handbook of Theory and Research,* vol. 3, edited by John C. Smart. New York: Agathon Press.

Fisher, James L. 1984. *The Power of the Presidency.* New York: Macmillan.

Fisher, James L., Martha W. Tack, and Karen J. Wheeler. 1988. "Leadership Behaviors of Effective College Presidents." Paper presented at an annual meeting of the American Educational Research Association, April, New Orleans, Louisiana.

Floyd, Carol E. 1985. *Faculty Participation in Decision Making: Necessity or Luxury?* ASHE-ERIC Higher Education Report No. 8. Washington, D.C.: Association for the Study of Higher Education. ED 267 694. 119 pp. MF–01; PC–05.

French, John R.P., Jr., and Bertram Raven. 1968. "The Bases of Social Power." In *Group Dynamics: Research and Theory,* edited by Dorwin Cartwright and Alvin Zander. 3d ed. New York: Harper & Row.

Frieze, Irene, and Bernard Weiner. 1971. "Cue Utilization and Attributional Judgments for Success and Failure." *Journal of Personality* 39: 591–606.

Gardner, John W. 1986a. "The Heart of the Matter: Leader-Constituent Interaction." Third in a series of papers prepared for the Leadership Studies Program. Washington, D.C.: Leadership Studies Program.

———. 1986b. "Leadership and Power." Fourth in a series of papers prepared for the Leadership Studies Program. Washington, D.C.: Leadership Studies Program.

———. 1986c. "The Moral Aspect of Leadership." Fifth in a series of papers prepared for the Leadership Studies Program. Washington, D.C.: Leadership Studies Program.

———. 1986d. "The Nature of Leadership." First in a series of papers prepared for the Leadership Studies Program. Washington, D.C.: Leadership Studies Program.

———. 1986e. "The Tasks of Leadership." Second in a series of papers prepared for the Leadership Studies Program. Washington, D.C.: Leadership Studies Program.

———. 1987a. "Attributes and Context." Sixth in a series of papers prepared for the Leadership Studies Program. Washington, D.C.: Leadership Studies Program.

———. 1987b. "Constituents and Followers." Eighth in a series of papers prepared for the Leadership Studies Program. Washington, D.C.: Leadership Studies Program.

———. 1987c. "Leadership Development." Seventh in a series of papers prepared for the Leadership Studies Program. Washington, D.C.: Leadership Studies Program.

———. 1988a. "The Changing Nature of Leadership." Eleventh in a series of papers prepared for the Leadership Studies Program. Washington, D.C.: Leadership Studies Program.

———. 1988b. "Renewing: The Leader's Creative Task." Tenth in a series of papers prepared for the Leadership Studies Program. Washington, D.C.: Leadership Studies Program.

———. 1988c. "The Task of Motivating." Ninth in a series of papers prepared for the Leadership Studies Program. Washington, D.C.: Leadership Studies Program.

Gibb, Cecil A. 1968. "Leadership." In *The Handbook of Social Psychology,* vol. 4, edited by Gardner Lindzey and Elliot Aronson. 3d ed. Reading, Mass.: Addison-Wesley.

Gilley, J.W., Kenneth A. Fulmer, and S.J. Reithlingshoefer. 1986. *Searching for Academic Excellence: Twenty Colleges on the Move and Their Leaders.* New York: American Council on Education/ Macmillan.

Goodman, Paul. 1962. *The Community of Scholars.* New York: Random House.

Green, Madeleine F., ed. 1988a. "The American College President: A Contemporary Profile." Washington, D.C.: American Council on Education.

———. 1988b. *Leaders for a New Era: Strategies for Higher Education.* New York: American Council on Education/Macmillan.

Green S.G., and T.R. Mitchell. 1979. "Attributional Processes of Leaders in Leader-Member Interactions." *Organizational Behavior and Human Performance* 23: 429–58.

Greene, Charles N. 1975. "The Reciprocal Nature of Influence between Leader and Subordinate." *Journal of Applied Psychology* 60(2): 187–93.

———. 1979. "Questions of Causation in the Path-Goal Theory of Leadership." *Academy of Management Journal* 22: 22–41.

Hammond, Martine F. 1981. "Organizational Response for Survival: A Case Study in Higher Education." Paper presented at the annual meeting of the Association for the Study of Higher Education, March. ED 203 811. 25 pp. MF–01; PC–01.

Hersey, P., and K.H. Blanchard. 1977. *Management of Organizational Behavior.* 3d ed. Englewood Cliffs, N. J.: Prentice-Hall.

Hesburgh, Theodore. May-June 1979. "The College Presidency: Life between a Rock and a Hard Place." *Change* 11: 43–47.

Hills, F.S., and T.A. Mahoney. 1978. "University Budgets and Organizational Decision Making." *Administrative Science Quarterly* 23: 454–65.

Hollander, Edwin P. 1964. *Leaders, Groups, and Influence.* New York: Oxford Univ. Press.

———. 1985. "Leadership and Power" In *The Handbook of Social Psychology,* edited by G. Lindzey and E. Aronson. 3d ed. New York: Random House.

————. May 1987. "College and University Leadership from a Social Psychological Perspective: A Transactional View." Prepared for the Invitational Interdisciplinary Colloquium on Leadership in Higher Education, sponsored by the Institutional Leadership Project, National Center for Postsecondary Governance and Finance, Teachers College, New York City.

Homans, George C. 1950. *The Human Group.* New York: Harcourt, Brace & World.

————. 1958. "Social Behavior as Exchange." *American Journal of Sociology* 63: 597–606.

————. 1961. *Social Behavior: Its Elementary Forms.* New York: Harcourt, Brace & World.

House, Robert J. 1971. "A Path-Goal Theory of Leader Effectiveness." *Administrative Science Quarterly* 16: 321–38.

House, Robert J., and Mary L. Baetz. 1979. "Leadership: Some Empirical Generalizations and New Research Directions." *Research in Organizational Behavior* 1: 341–423.

Howell, Jon P., and Peter W. Dorfman. 1981. "Substitutes for Leadership: Test of a Construct." *Academy of Management Journal* 24(4): 714–28.

Howell, Jon P., Peter W. Dorfman, and Steven Kerr. 1986. "Moderator Variables in Leadership Research." *Academy of Management Review* 11(1): 88–102.

Jacobson, Robert L. 20 May 1985. "Trustees Vexed over Colleges' Quality, Said to Mull Role in Academic Affairs." *Chronicle of Higher Education* 29(23): 1+.

Kahneman, D., P. Slovic, and A. Tversky. 1982. *Judgment under Uncertainty: Heuristics and Biases.* Cambridge: Cambridge Univ. Press.

Kanter, Rosabeth Moss. 1983. *The Change Masters.* New York: Simon & Schuster, Inc.

Kaplowitz, Richard A. 1986. *Selecting College and University Personnel: The Quest and the Question.* ASHE-ERIC Higher Education Report No. 8. Washington, D.C.: Association for the Study of Higher Education. ED 282 488. 121 pp. MF–01; PC–05.

Kast, Fremont E., and James E. Rosenzweig, eds. 1973. *Contingency Views of Organization and Management.* Chicago: Science Research Associates.

Katz, Daniel, and Robert L. Kahn. 1978. *The Social Psychology of Organizations.* 2d ed. New York: John Wiley & Sons.

Kauffman, Joseph F. 1980. *At the Pleasure of the Board: The Service of the College and University President.* Washington, D.C.: American Council on Education. ED 187 217. 122 pp. MF-01; PC not available EDRS.

Keeton, Morris. 1971. *Shared Authority on Campus.* Washington, D.C.: American Association for Higher Education.

Keller, George. 1983. *Academic Strategy: The Management Revolution in American Higher Education*. Baltimore: Johns Hopkins Univ. Press.

Kellerman, Barbara. October 1987. "The Politics of Leadership in America: Implications for Higher Education in the Late 20th Century." Prepared for the Invitational Interdisciplinary Colloquium on Leadership in Higher Education, sponsored by the Institutional Leadership Project, National Center for Postsecondary Governance and Finance, Teachers College, New York City.

Keohane, Nanneri. 1985. "Collaboration and Leadership: Are They in Conflict?" *College Board Review 135: 4–5+*.

Kerr, Clark. 1963. *The Uses of the University*. Cambridge, Mass.: Harvard Univ. Press.

———. 1984. *Presidents Make a Difference: Strengthening Leadership in Colleges and Universities*. Washington, D.C.: Association of Governing Boards of Universities and Colleges. ED 247 879. 140 pp. MF–01; PC not available EDRS.

Kerr, Clark, and Marian Gade. 1986. *The Many Lives of Academic Presidents*. Washington, D.C.: Association of Governing Boards of Universities and Colleges. ED 267 704. 267 pp. MF–01; PC–11.

Kerr, Steven, and John M. Jermier. 1978. "Substitutes for Leadership: Their Meaning and Measurement." *Organizational Behavior and Human Performance* 22: 375–403.

Knight, W. Hal, and Michael C. Holen. 1985. "Leadership and the Perceived Effectiveness of Department Chairpersons." *Journal of Higher Education* 56(6): 677–90.

Korman, Abraham K. 1966. " 'Consideration,' 'Initiating Structure,' and Organizational Criteria: A Review." *Personal Psychology* 19: 349–61.

Kuh, George D., and Elizabeth J. Whitt. 1988. *The Invisible Tapestry*. ASHE-ERIC Higher Education Report No. 1. Washington, D.C.: Association for the Study of Higher Education. HE 021 960. 144 pp. MF–01; PC–06.

Kuhn, Thomas S. 1970. "The Structure of Scientific Revolutions." *International Encyclopedia of Unified Science,* vol. 2, no. 2. 2d ed. Chicago: Univ. of Chicago Press.

Laney, James T. Spring 1984. "The Moral Authority of the College or University President." *Educational Record:* 17-19.

Lieberson, Stanley, and James F. O'Connor. 1972. "Leadership and Organizational Performance: A Study of Large Corporations." *American Sociological Review:* 37(2): 117-30.

Likert, Rensis. 1961. *New Patterns of Management*. New York: McGraw-Hill.

———. 1967. *The Human Organization*. New York: McGraw-Hill.

Lincoln, Yvonna, ed. 1985. *Organizational Theory and Inquiry: The Paradigm Revolution.* Beverly Hills, Calif.: Sage Publications.

Lindblom, Charles E. 1968. *The Policy-Making Process.* Englewood Cliffs, N.J.: Prentice-Hall.

Lippett, Ronald, and Ralph K. White. 1958. "An Experimental Study of Leadership and Group Life." In *Readings in Social Psychology,* edited by Eleanor MacCoby, Theodore M. Newcomb, and Eugene L. Hartley. 3d ed. New York: Holt, Rinehart & Winston.

Lunsford, T.F. 1970. "Authority and Ideology in the Administered University." In *The State of the University: Authority and Change,* edited by C.E. Kruytbosch and S.L. Messinger. Beverly Hills: Sage Publications.

McCall, Morgan W., Jr., and Michael M. Lombardo, eds. 1978. *Leadership: Where Else Can We Go?* Durham, N.C.: Duke Univ. Press.

McCorkle, Chester O., Jr., and Sandra O. Archibald. 1982. *Management and Leadership in Higher Education.* San Francisco: Jossey-Bass.

McElroy, J.C. 1982. "A Typology of Attribution Leadership Research." *Academy of Management Review* 7(3): 413–17.

McGregor, Douglas. 1960. *The Human Side of Enterprise.* New York: McGraw-Hill.

Machiavelli, Niccolo. 1977 (orig. pub. 1513). *The Prince,* translated and edited by Robert M. Adams. New York: W.W. Norton & Co.

McMillen, Liz. 4 June 1986. "Feud between President and Regents Debilitates University of New Mexico." *Chronicle of Higher Education* 32(14): 1+.

Madron, Thomas W., James R. Craig, and Raymond M. Mendel. 1976. "Departmental Morale as a Function of the Perceived Performance of Department Heads." *Research in Higher Education* 5: 83–94.

March, James G. 1982. "Emerging Developments in the Study of Organizations." *Review of Higher Education* 6: 1–18.

———. 1984. "How We Talk and How We Act: Administrative Theory and Administrative Life." In *Leadership and Organizational Culture,* edited by Thomas J. Sergiovanni and John E. Corbally. Urbana: Univ. of Illinois Press.

March, James G., and Johan P. Olsen. 1979. *Ambiguity and Choice in Organizations.* 2d ed. Bergen, Norway: Universitetsforlaget.

March, James G., and Herbert A. Simon. 1958. *Organizations.* New York: John Wiley & Sons.

Martin, Joanne. 1982. "Stories and Scripts in Organizational Settings." In *Cognitive Social Psychology,* edited by Albert H. Hastorf and Alice M. Isen. New York: Elsevier N. Holland.

Martin, J., M.S. Feldman, M.J. Hatch, and S.S. Sitkin. 1983. "The Uniqueness Paradox in Organizational Stories." *Administrative Science Quarterly* 28: 438-53.

Mayhew, Lewis B. 1979. *Surviving the Eighties.* San Francisco: Jossey-Bass.

Meindl, James R., Sanford B. Ehrlich, and Janet M. Dukerich. 1985. "The Romance of Leadership." *Administrative Science Quarterly* 30: 78–102.

Meyer, John W., and Brian Rowan. 1983. "Institutionalized Organizations: Formal Structure as Myth and Ceremony." In *Organizational Environments: Ritual and Rationality,* edited by John W. Meyer and W.R. Scott. Beverly Hills: Sage Publications.

Millett, John D. 1962. *An Essay on Organization: The Academic Community.* New York: McGraw-Hill.

———. 1974. *Strengthening Community in Higher Education.* Washington, D.C.: Management Division, Academy for Educational Development, Inc.

———. 1978. *New Structures of Campus Power: Success and Failures of Emerging Forms of Institutional Governance.* San Francisco: Jossey-Bass.

Mintzberg, Henry. 1973. *The Nature of Managerial Work.* New York: Harper & Row.

Mitchell, Terence, James R. Larson, and S.G. Green. 1977. "Leader Behavior, Situational Moderators, and Group Performance: An Attributional Analysis." *Organizational Behavior and Human Performance* 18: 254–68.

Mooney, Carolyn J. 13 July 1988. "For College Presidents, a Loss of Faculty Confidence Can Lead to War—or Dialogue." *Chronicle of Higher Education* 34(44): A1+.

Morgan, Gareth. 1986. *Images of Organization.* Beverly Hills: Sage Publications.

Mortimer, Kenneth P., and T.R. McConnell. 1978. *Sharing Authority Effectively: Participation, Interaction, and Discretion.* San Francisco: Jossey-Bass.

National Institute of Education, Study Group on the Conditions of Excellence in American Higher Education. 1984. *Involvement in Learning: Realizing the Potential of American Higher Education.* Washington, D.C.: Author. ED 275 951. 22 pp. MF-01; PC-01.

Neumann, Anna. 1987. "Defining 'Good Faculty Leadership': Interpretations of Professors and Presidents." Paper presented at an annual meeting of the Association for the Study of Higher Education, November, Baltimore, Maryland. ED 292 394. 28 pp. MF–01; PC–02.

———. 1988. "Making Mistakes: Error and Learning in the College Presidency." Paper presented at an annual meeting of the American Educational Research Association, April, New Orleans, Louisiana. ED 298 810. 26 pp. MF–01; PC–02.

———. 1989a. "Colleges under Pressure: Budgeting, Presidential Competence, and Faculty Uncertainty." Paper presented at an annual meeting of the American Educational Research Association, March, San Francisco, California.

———. 1989b. "Strategic Leadership: The Changing Orientations of College Presidents." *The Review of Higher Education* 12: 137–51. ED 292 393. 21 pp. MF–01; PC–01.

Nisbett, R., and L. Ross. 1980. *Human Inference: Strategies and Shortcomings of Social Judgment.* Englewood Cliffs: Prentice-Hall.

Peck, Robert D. 1983. "The Entrepreneurial College Presidency." *Educational Record* 64: 18–25.

Perkins, J.A., ed. 1973. *The University as an Organization.* New York: McGraw-Hill.

Perrow, Charles. 1979. *Complex Organizations: A Critical Essay.* 2d ed. Glenview, Ill.: Scott, Foresman & Co.

Peters, Thomas J., and Robert H. Waterman. 1982. *In Search of Excellence: Lessons from America's Best-Run Companies.* New York: Harper & Row.

Peterson, Marvin W. March 1985. "Emerging Developments in Postsecondary Organization Theory and Research: Fragmentation or Integration." *Educational Researcher* 14: 5–12.

Pfeffer, Jeffrey. 1977. "The Ambiguity of Leadership." *Academy of Management Review* 2: 104–12.

———. 1978. "The Ambiguity of Leadership." In *Leadership: Where Else Can We Go?* edited by M. McCall and M. Lombardo. Durham, N.C.: Duke Univ.

———. 1981. "Management as Symbolic Action: The Creation and Maintenance of Organizational Paradigms." *Research in Organizational Behavior* 3: 1–52.

Pfeffer, Jeffrey, and Gerald R. Salancik. 1978. *The External Control of Organizations: A Resource Dependency Perspective.* New York: Harper & Row.

Phillips, J.S., and Robert G. Lord. 1981. "Causal Attributions and Perceptions of Leadership." *Organizational Behavior and Human Performance* 28: 143–63.

Plante, Patricia R. 29 May 1985. "The College Administrator in the Marketplace." *Chronicle of Higher Education* 30(13): 72.

Powers, David R., and Mary F. Powers. 1983. *Making Participatory Management Work.* San Francisco: Jossey-Bass.

Price, Kenneth H., and Howard Garland. 1981. "Compliance with a Leader's Suggestions as a Function of Perceived Leader/Member Competence and Potential Reciprocity." *Journal of Applied Psychology* 66(3): 329–36.

Quinn, Robert E. 1988. *Beyond Rational Management: Mastering the Paradoxes and Competing Demands of High Performance.* San Francisco: Jossey-Bass.

Reyes, P., and S.B. Twombly. Winter 1987. "Perceptions of Contemporary Governance in Community Colleges: An Empirical Study."

Community College Review 14: 4–12.

Rice, R. Eugene, and Ann E. Austin. March/April 1988. "High Faculty Morale: What Exemplary Colleges Do Right." *Change* 20: 51–58.

Richardson, Richard C., ed. 1975. *Reforming College Governance.* New Directions for Community Colleges No. 10. San Francisco: Jossey-Bass.

Richardson, Richard C., Jr., Clyde E. Blocker, and Louis W. Bender. 1972. *Governance for the Two-Year College.* Englewood Cliffs, N.J.: Prentice-Hall.

Richardson, Richard C., and William R. Rhodes. 1983. "Building Commitment to the Institution." In *Issues for Community College Leaders in a New Era,* edited by George B. Vaughan and Associates. San Francisco: Jossey-Bass.

Richman, Barry M., and Richard N. Farmer. 1976. *Leadership, Goals, and Power in Higher Education.* San Francisco: Jossey-Bass.

Riesman, David, and Sharon Elliott Fuller. 1985. "Leaders: Presidents Who Make a Difference." In *Opportunity in Adversity,* edited by Janice S. Green, Arthur Levine, and Associates. San Francisco: Jossey-Bass.

Salancik, Gerald R., and J.R. Meindl. 1984. "Corporate Attributions as Strategic Illusions of Management Control." *Administrative Science Quarterly* 29: 238–54.

Salancik, Gerald R., and Jeffrey Pfeffer. 1974. "The Bases and Use of Power in Organizational Decision Making: The Case of a University." *Administrative Science Quarterly* 19: 453–73.

———. 1977. "Constraints on Administrator Discretion: The Limited Influence of Mayors on City Budgets." *Urban Affairs Quarterly* 12(4): 475–98.

Sayles, Leonard R. 1979. *Leadership: What Effective Managers Really Do...and How They Do It.* New York: McGraw-Hill.

Schein, Edgar H. 1985. *Organizational Culture and Leadership.* San Francisco: Jossey-Bass.

Scott, W. Richard. 1981. *Organizations: Rational, Natural, and Open Systems.* Englewood Cliffs, N.J.: Prentice-Hall.

Selznick, Philip. 1957. *Leadership in Administration: A Sociological Interpretation.* New York: Harper & Row.

Sergiovanni, Thomas J., and John E. Corbally, eds. 1984. *Leadership and Organizational Culture.* Chicago: Univ. of Illinois Press.

Silverman, Robert J. 1987. "How We Know What We Know: A Study of Higher Education Journal Articles." *Review of Higher Education* 11(1): 39–59.

Sims, Henry P., Dennis A. Gioia, and Associates. 1986. *The Thinking Organization: Dynamics of Organizational Thinking Cognition.* San Francisco: Jossey-Bass.

Smircich, Linda. 1983. "Concepts of Culture and Organizational Analysis." *Administrative Science Quarterly* 28: 339-58.

Smircich, Linda, and Gareth Morgan. 1982. "Leadership: The Management of Meaning." *Journal of Applied Behavioral Science* 18(3): 257–73.

Srivastra, Suresh, and Associates. 1983. *The Executive Mind.* San Francisco: Jossey-Bass.

Staw, B.M. 1975. "Attribution of the Causes of Performance: A New Alternative Explanation of Cross-sectional Research on Organizations." *Organizational Behavior and Human Performance* 13: 414–32.

Staw, Barry M. 1983. "Motivation Research versus the Art of Faculty Management." *The Review of Higher Education* 6(4): 301–21.

Steinbruner, J.D. 1974. *The Cybernetic Theory of Decision.* Princeton, N.J.: Princeton Univ. Press.

Stogdill, R.M., and A.E. Coons. 1957. *Leader Behavior: Its Description and Measurement.* Columbus: Ohio State Univ., Bureau of Business Research.

Stroup, Herbert. 1966. *Bureaucracy in Higher Education.* New York: Free Press.

Taylor, Alton L. 1982. "Decision-Process Behaviors of Academic Managers." *Research in Higher Education* 16(2): 155–73.

Tierney, William G. 1985. "Leadership and Organizational Culture in Public State Colleges." Unpublished paper. National Center for Higher Education Management Systems.

———. 1988. "Organizational Culture in Higher Education." *Journal of Higher Education* 59(1): 2–21.

———. 1989. "Symbolism and Presidential Perceptions of Leadership." *Review of Higher Education* 12: 153–66.

Trow, Martin A. 1984. *The University Presidency: Comparative Reflections on Leadership.* Urbana: Univ. of Illinois-Urbana/Champaign.

———. 1985. "Comparative Reflections on Leadership in Higher Education." *European Journal of Education* 20: 2–3+.

Tucker, Allan. 1981. *Chairing the Academic Department: Leadership among Peers.* Washington, D.C.: American Council on Education.

Vaughan, George B. 1986. *The Community College President.* New York: American Council on Education/Macmillan.

Vroom, Victor H. 1976. "Leadership." In *Handbook of Industrial and Organizational Psychology,* edited by M. Dunnette. Chicago: Rand McNally.

———. 1983. "Leaders and Leadership in Academe." *Review of Higher Education* 6(4): 367–86.

Vroom, Victor H., and Phillip W. Yetton. 1973. *Leadership and Decision Making.* Pittsburgh: Univ. of Pittsburgh Press.

Walker, Donald. 1979. *The Effective Administrator: A Practical Approach to Problem Solving, Decision Making, and Campus Leadership.* San Francisco: Jossey-Bass.

Ward, Alex. 12 June 1988. "Monk Malloy's Notre Dame." *New York Times Magazine.*

Weber, Max. 1947. "The Essentials of Bureaucratic Organization: An Ideal-Type Construction." In *The Theory of Social and Economic Organization,* edited by Talcott Parsons. London: Oxford Univ. Press.

Weick, Karl E. 1976. "Educational Organizations as Loosely Coupled Systems." *Administrative Science Quarterly* 21: 1–19.

———. 1979. *The Social Psychology of Organizing.* New York: Random House.

———. 1982. "Administering Education in Loosely Coupled Schools." *Phi Delta Kappan* 63(10): 673–76.

Weiner, Bernard. 1985. " 'Spontaneous' Causal Thinking." *Psychological Bulletin* 97(1): 74–84.

Weiner, Bernard, and Andy Kukla. 1970. "An Attributional Analysis of Achievement Motivation." *Journal of Personality and Social Psychology* 15(1): 1–20.

Whetten, David A. 1984. "Effective Administrators: Good Management on the College Campus." *Change* 16(8): 38–43.

Whetten, David A., and Kim S. Cameron. 1985. "Administrative Effectiveness in Higher Education." *Review of Higher Education* 9(11): 35–49.

Yukl, Gary A. 1971. "Toward a Behavioral Theory of Leadership." *Organizational Behavior and Human Performance* 6: 414–40.

———. 1981. *Leadership in Organizations.* Englewood Cliffs, N.J.: Prentice-Hall.

Zahn, Lawrence G., and Gerrit Wolf. 1981. "Leadership and the Art of Cycle Maintenance: A Simulation Model of Superior-Subordinate Interaction." *Organizational Behavior and Human Performance* 28: 26–49.

INDEX

A

AAUP (see American Association of University Professors)
Academic administration models, 43
Academic Strategy, 1
Adaptive strategies, 47, 64, 65
Adversity, 42, 43
American Association of University Professors (AAUP), 2–3
Anarchy model, 31, 40
Antioch College, 46, 50
"Atomistic model," 62
Authoritarian leadership, 12
Authoritarian-democratic leadership, 12
Authority-obedience style, 43

B

Behavioral theories, 7, 12–14, 43–46
Bennett, William, 1
Blue ribbon commissions, 1
Bureaucracy
       model, 26, 28, 33
       university as, 51–54

C

Caretaker style, 43
Catalytic leaders, 58
Change
       radical, 74
       reaction to, 42
       strategies for, 48
Charisma, 24, 38–39
Chronicle of Higher Education, 3
Churchill, Winston, 42
Clark, Burton, 50
Coalitions
       formation of, 30, 38
       organizations as, 29
Coercive power, 9
Cognitive theories, 7, 16, 23–24, 49
Cognitive complexity, 65, 72–73
Collegial model, 54–57
Comfortable-pleasant style, 43
Committee chairs, 57
Communication
       networks, 79
       processes, 55–56
Community colleges
       faculty leadership, 56

N

Neutralizer characteristics, 19

O

Ohio State leadership studies, 13, 14, 35
Organizational characteristics, 19–20
Organizational control, 9
Organizational culture, 21–22, 43, 46–49
Organizational theory
        and higher education, 51–67
        and images of leadership, 26–33
"Organized anarchy," 31, 32, 60–62, 77

P

Paridigms, 76
Participatory processes, 56
Path-goal theory, 17, 45
People orientation, 43
Perception of leadership, 25–26, 55–56
Persistence, 60
Personal attributes, 8, 35
Personnel selection, 64
Political frame, 27, 29–31, 57–59
Power
        blocs, 59
        coercive, 9
        faculty/trustee, 39
        political use of, 30
        referent, 9, 38
        sources of, 38
Power/influence theories
        leadership model, 7, 8–12
        social exchange, 39–40
        social power, 37–39
        transactional, 39–40
        transformational, 40–43
Presidents
        advice to, 5–6
        as center of power, 51, 55
        bureaucratic, 53
        collegial systems, 55
        control over resources, 4–5
        cooperation with faulty/trustees/constituents, 3
        effective, 36, 55
        experienced, 66
        heroic image, 51–52
        new, 39-40, 43, 44, 66

past, 4
perception of role, 43–44
pressures on, 3
successful vs. unsuccessful, 72
transformational, 41–42
Private colleges: faculty leadership, 56
Problem-solving, 59

R

Reed College, 46, 50
Relationship orientation, 13, 16
Research on leadership
    agenda, 78–80
    multidimensional, 80
    narrowly focused studies, 80
    new trends, 69–70
    relevance, 69
Resources
    allocation of scarce, 29, 30
    organizational influence, 30
Revitalization of colleges, 1
Rewards
    control over, 19
    faculty, 74
    power, 9

S

Search committees, 4
Situational leadership theory, 17
Situational variables, 14, 15, 19, 44
Small colleges: faculty leadership, 56
Social exchange theory, 8, 39–40, 72, 74
Social power theory, 8, 37–39
Socialization, 72
Stalin, 39
State colleges
    collegial approach, 57
    faculty leadership, 56
Status, 60
"Strong" leadership, 77
Structural frame, 27, 28–29, 51–54
Student satisfaction, 53
Style
    identification, 13
    related to faculty/student outcomes, 44
    types, 43
Substitutes for hierarchical leadership, 19, 20, 46, 50, 79

ASHE-ERIC HIGHER EDUCATION REPORTS

Since 1983, the Association for the Study of Higher Education (ASHE) and the Educational Resources Information Center (ERIC) Clearinghouse on Higher Education, a sponsored project of the School of Education and Human Development at The George Washington University, have cosponsored the *ASHE-ERIC Higher Education Report* series. The 1989 series is the eighteenth overall and the first to be published by the School of Education and Human Development at the George Washington University.

Each monograph is the definitive analysis of a tough higher education problem, based on thorough research of pertinent literature and insitutional experiences. Topics are identified by a national survey. Noted practitioners and scholars are then commissioned to write the reports, with experts providing critical reviews of each manuscript before publication.

Eight monographs (10 before 1985) in the *ASHE-ERIC Higher Education Report* series are published each year and are available on a individual or subscription basis. Subscription to eight issues is $80.00 annually; $60 to members of AAHE, AIR, or AERA; and $50 to ASHE members. All foreign subscribers must include an additional $10 per series year for postage.

Prices for single copies, including book rate postage, are $15.00 regular and $11.25 for members of AERA, AIR, AAHE, and ASHE ($10.00 regular and $7.50 for members for 1985 to 1987 reports, $7.50 regular and $6.00 for members for 1983 and 1984 reports, $6.50 regular and $5.00 for members for reports published before 1982). All foreign orders must include $1.00 per book for foreign postage. Fast United Parcel Service or first class postage is available for $1.00 per book in the U.S. and $2.50 per book outside the U.S. (orders above $50.00 may substitue 5% of the total invoice amount for domestic postage). Make checks payable to ASHE-ERIC. For VISA and MasterCard payments, include card number, expiration date, and signature. Orders under $25 must be prepaid. Bulk discounts are available on orders of 15 or more reports (not applicable to subscription orders). Order from the Publications Department, *ASHE-ERIC Higher Education Reports,* The George Washington University, One Dupont Circle, Suite 630, Washington, DC 20036-1183, or phone us at (202) 296-2597. Write for a complete catalog of all available reports.

1989 ASHE-ERIC Higher Education Reports

1. Making Sense of Administrative Leadership: The 'L' Word in Higher Education
   Estela M. Bensimon, Anna Neumann, and Robert Birnbaum

1988 ASHE-ERIC Higher Education Reports

1. The Invisible Tapestry: Culture in American Colleges and Universities
   George D. Kuh and Elizabeth J. Whitt

2. Critical Thinking: Theory, Research, Practice, and Possibilities
   Joanne Gainen Kurfiss

3. Developing Academic Programs: The Climate for Innovation
   Daniel T. Seymour

4. Peer Teaching: To Teach is To Learn Twice
   Neal A. Whitman

5. Higher Education and State Governments: Renewed Partnership, Cooperation, or Competition?
   Edward R. Hines

6. Entrepreneurship and Higher Education: Lessons for Colleges, Universities, and Industry
   James S. Fairweather

7. Planning for Microcomputers in Higher Education: Strategies for the Next Generation
   Reynolds Ferrante, John Hayman, Mary Susan Carlson, and Harry Phillips

8. The Challenge for Research in Higher Education: Harmonizing Excellence and Utility
   Alan W. Lindsay and Ruth T. Neumann

1987 ASHE-ERIC Higher Education Reports

1. Incentive Early Retirement Programs for Faculty: Innovative Responses to a Changing Environment
   Jay L. Chronister and Thomas R. Kepple, Jr.

2. Working Effectively with Trustees: Building Cooperative Campus Leadership
   Barbara E. Taylor

3. Formal Recognition of Employer-Sponsored Instruction: Conflict and Collegiality in Postsecondary Education
   Nancy S. Nash and Elizabeth M. Hawthorne

4. Learning Styles: Implications for Improving Educational Practices
   Charles S. Claxton and Patricia H. Murrell

5. Higher Education Leadership: Enhancing Skills through Professional Development Programs
   Sharon A. McDade

6. Higher Education and the Public Trust: Improving Stature in Colleges and Universities
   Richard L. Alfred and Julie Weissman

7. College Student Outcomes Assessment: A Talent Development Perspective
   Maryann Jacobi, Alexander Astin, and Frank Ayala, Jr.

8. Opportunity from Strength: Strategic Planning Clarified with Case Examples
   Robert G. Cope

1986 ASHE-ERIC Higher Education Reports

1. Post-tenure Faculty Evaluation: Threat or Opportunity?
   Christine M. Licata

2. Blue Ribbon Commissions and Higher Education: Changing Academe from the Outside
   Janet R. Johnson and Laurence R. Marcus

3. Responsive Professional Education: Balancing Outcomes and Opportunities
   Joan S. Stark, Malcolm A. Lowther, and Bonnie M.K. Hagerty

4. Increasing Students' Learning: A Faculty Guide to Reducing Stress among Students
   Neal A. Whitman, David C. Spendlove, and Claire H. Clark

5. Student Financial Aid and Women: Equity Dilemma?
   Mary Moran

6. The Master's Degree: Tradition, Diversity, Innovation
   Judith S. Glazer

7. The College, the Constitution, and the Consumer Student: Implications for Policy and Practice
   Robert M. Hendrickson and Annette Gibbs

8. Selecting College and University Personnel: The Quest and the Question
   Richard A. Kaplowitz

1985 ASHE-ERIC Higher Education Reports

1. Flexibility in Academic Staffing: Effective Policies and Practices
   Kenneth P. Mortimer, Marque Bagshaw, and Andrew T. Masland

2. Associations in Action: The Washington, D.C. Higher Education Community
   Harland G. Bloland

3. And on the Seventh Day: Faculty Consulting and Supplemental Income
   Carol M. Boyer and Darrell R. Lewis

4. Faculty Research Performance: Lessons from the Sciences and Social Sciences
   John W. Creswell

5. Academic Program Review: Institutional Approaches, Expectations, and Controversies
   Clifton F. Conrad and Richard F. Wilson

6. Students in Urban Settings: Achieving the Baccalaureate Degree
   Richard C. Richardson, Jr. and Louis W. Bender

7. Serving More Than Students: A Critical Need for College Student Personnel Services
   Peter H. Garland

8. Faculty Participation in Decision Making: Necessity or Luxury?
   Carol E. Floyd

1984 ASHE-ERIC Higher Education Reports

1. Adult Learning: State Policies and Institutional Practices
   K. Patricia Cross and Anne-Marie McCartan

2. Student Stress: Effects and Solutions
   Neal A. Whitman, David C. Spendlove, and Claire H. Clark

3. Part-time Faulty: Higher Education at a Crossroads
   Judith M. Gappa

4. Sex Discrimination Law in Higher Education: The Lessons of the Past Decade
   J. Ralph Lindgren, Patti T. Ota, Perry A. Zirkel, and Nan Van Gieson

5. Faculty Freedoms and Institutional Accountability: Interactions and Conflicts
   Steven G. Olswang and Barbara A. Lee

6. The High Technology Connection: Academic/Industrial Cooperation for Economic Growth
   Lynn G. Johnson

7. Employee Educational Programs: Implications for Industry and Higher Education
   Suzanne W. Morse

8. Academic Libraries: The Changing Knowledge Centers of Colleges and Universities
   Barbara B. Moran

9. Futures Research and the Strategic Planning Process: Implications for Higher Education
   James L. Morrison, William L. Renfro, and Wayne I. Boucher

10. Faculty Workload: Research, Theory, and Interpretation
    Harold E. Yuker

1983 ASHE-ERIC Higher Education Reports

1. The Path to Excellence: Quality Assurance in Higher Education
   Laurence R. Marcus, Anita O. Leone, and Edward D. Goldberg

2. Faculty Recruitment, Retention, and Fair Employment: Obligations and Opportunities
   John S. Waggaman

3. Meeting the Challenges: Developing Faculty Careers*
   Michael C.T. Brooks and Katherine L. German

4. Raising Academic Standards: A Guide to Learning Improvement
   Ruth Talbott Keimig

5. Serving Learners at a Distance: A Guide to Program Practices
   Charles E. Feasley

6. Competence, Admissions, and Articulation: Returning to the Basics in Higher Education
   Jean L. Preer

7. Public Service in Higher Education: Practices and Priorities
   Patricia H. Crosson

8. Academic Employment and Retrenchment: Judicial Review and Administrative Action
   Robert M. Hendrickson and Barbara A. Lee

9. Burnout: The New Academic Disease*
   Winifred Albizu Meléndez and Rafael M. de Guzmán

10. Academic Workplace: New Demands, Heightened Tensions
    Ann E. Austin and Zelda F. Gamson

*Out-of-print. Available through EDRS. Call 1-800-227-ERIC.
